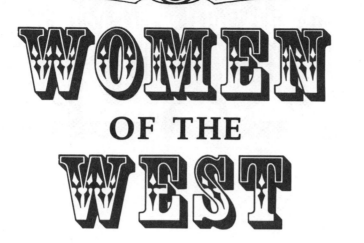

WOMEN
OF THE
WEST

WOMEN

OF THE WEST

BY SILVIA ANNE SHEAFER

 **ADDISON-WESLEY**

Copyright © 1980, 1979, 1978 by Silvia Anne Sheafer
All Rights Reserved
Addison-Wesley Publishing Company, Inc.
Reading, Massachusetts 01867
Printed in the United States of America
ABCDEFGHIJK-DO-89876543210

Library of Congress Cataloging in Publication Data
Sheafer, Silvia Anne.
Women of the West.

   "This material was first published in two volumes:
Frontier women and Gold rush women, by Silvia Anne
Sheafer."
   SUMMARY: Brief sketches of a variety of western
women of the 1800's. Illustrated with graphics of
the period.
   1.   Women—The West—Biography—Juvenile litera-
ture.   2.   The West—Social life-and customs—
Juvenile literature.   [1.   The West—Biography]
I.   Title.
HQ1412.S52   305.4'092'2 [920]   79-28447
ISBN 0-201-06670-X

ISBN 0-201-06671-8 pbk.

Acknowledgments

Illustrations in this book are reproduced courtesy of the following:
page 4, 5: *The Gold Bug*, Alama, California
pages 6, 67, 136, 149: California State Library
pages 12, 18, 58, 141, 144: California Historical Society Library
page 20: U. S. Military Academy Archives
pages i, ii-iii, opposite 1, 22, 26, 34, 53, 65, 70, 78, 106, 113, 123, 124, 125:
    Wells Fargo Historical Archives
page 31: Bancroft Library
pages 3, 36, 40–41: Library of Congress
pages 46–47: Tom Myers, Bodie State Historic Park
page 50: Metropolitan Museum of Art, Gift of I. N. Phelps Stockes,
    Edward S. Hawes, Alice Mary Hawes, Marion Augusta Hawes, 1937
page 81: Levi Strauss & Co.
pages 88–89, 90, 97, 104, 109: Nevada County Historical Society
page 111: Southern Pacific Railroad
pages 120, 126–127: Amon Carter Museum, Fort Worth, Texas
page 43: lithograph published by Britton & Rev. of San Francisco

FOREWORD

Following the discovery of gold in California in 1847, gold seekers came by the thousands; Mexicans from the South, Chinese from the West, European immigrants from the East. By 1850 there was in excess of 380,000 pioneers of which only eight percent were women, all seeking their fortunes.

The first rush of people came mostly for gold, little more. And they traveled long and arduously to reach the West. In the beginning, they came across the Isthmus of Panama, fighting disease and jungle, sailing up the coast of Lower California, finally debarking at San Francisco, Before long, stage coaches and wagon trains were heading overland, battling highwaymen and Indians. And at last a great railroad was constructed linking the Atlantic and the Pacific.

Perhaps, the most complex newcomers were the women. They came to California for many reasons, none of which was to dig for gold. The famous historian Hubert Howe Bancroft wrote:

> *"The influence of women was strikingly exhibited in California mining camps. A hush would fall upon the reveling miners at the appearance of a woman in their secluded haunts. A chivalrous respect surrounded her wherever she moved, and she could travel alone throughout the land assured of respect and protection."*

Such glowing prose about women and their sudden arrival in gold camps is romantic to read, but not necessarily true. Some came West to be with their

v

husbands, others to seek marriage; the more ambitious sought theatrical careers. The frail or weaker women, unable to cope with extreme hardship, often fell in the turmoil. Those with a talent for writing sent messages home, inscribing forever the events of frontier life.

In time women were the dominant force in establishing Victorian values that smoothed away some of the raw edges of the period. But during the gaudy, reckless days of the Gold Rush, a woman's lot was not as easy as Bancroft would have us believe. In the following accounts, gathered together from newspapers of the day, historical records and personal journals, the plight of women is often seen as tragic or pathetic but always courageous.

This is their story.

CONTENTS

LOTTA CRABTREE

FAIRY STAR OF THE MOTHER LODE

A warm, lazy wind skirted across the green hills and picturesque ravines of northern California on a sleepy summer day in 1853. The previous night's scandalous activities were barely noticeable in the mining camp. Instead, heavy scents of sage, scrub oak, and pine penetrated the valley, and the occasional, everyday sounds of domesticated animals and camp gossip mingled in the dry quiet. But today was to be different.

In the shade of the blacksmith shop, a small crowd of men, several women, and some children had gathered. Dusty-booted and unwashed, the excited '49ers leaned on railings or against barn doors or trees, drinking and cheering the tiny attraction that had suddenly changed their routine.

Perched atop an iron anvil, a pretty little red-haired 6-year-old was dancing to the rhythm of clapping hands. Fine-featured, with sparkling brown eyes, Lotta Mignon Crabtree kicked her tiny heels and flicked the hem of her muslin skirts.

On the whim of her dancing teacher, a man called Bowers, these two unlikely inhabitants of Grass Valley, California had journeyed three miles by muleback to the wild mining camp of Rough and Ready. Named by Mexican War veterans, now residents, the tent city drew its name from General Zachary Taylor, "Old Rough and Ready." Much gold, including an eighteen-pound nugget, had already been gleaned from its rich ground. But Bowers had other ideas.

1

He saw in the mining town the possibilities of finding extra cash as well as undiscovered talent. He could build his wealth with his precocious students.

In those days, a town played host to many small stock companies, including Fairy Stars (singing and dancing children) and one-man entertainers. Child actors roamed the Sierras in profusion. All of these people beat their way through the hazardous gold country, sometimes facing peril. And although the leap from star pupil to Fairy Star was limited to a few talented youths, the rewards were tempting enough to make them try. Girls were especially in demand. Their very presence in the isolated camps was enough to bring tears to the eyes of the lonely miners, most of whom had left their families far away in the east. Remembering their own children and the joys of parenthood made the audience hospitable and more supportive. Today was no exception.

Lotta continued to dance about the anvil surface, smiling brightly and bouncing mimicking the traveling performers she had seen in San Francisco. It was there that she and her mother, Mary Ann Crabtree, had been infected with the charm and abundant spirit of actors and actresses. Though she was but 6 years old, Lotta Crabtree had shown early talent and a desire to perform.

Life for Lotta began in New York City. Her mother, Mary Ann Livesley, had arrived in New York with her mother, sisters, and brothers in the 1830s. Her father had drowned at sea while trying to settle his family in India. Undaunted by this tragedy, Mary

CALIFORNIA.

Golden Regions.

EMIGRATION TO
CALIFORNIA !

Do you want to go to California! If so, go and join the Company who intend going out the middle of March, or 1st of April next, under the charge of the California Emigration Society, in a first-rate Clipper Ship. The Society agreeing to find places for all those who wish it upon their arrival in San Francisco. The voyage will probably be made in a few months.— Price of passage will be in the vicinity of

ONE HUNDRED DOLLARS !
CHILDREN IN PROPORTION.

A number of families have already engaged passage. A suitable Female Nurse has been provided, who will take charge of Young Ladies and Children. Good Physicians, both male and female go in the Ship. It is hoped a large number of females will go, as Females are getting almost as good wages as males.

FEMALE NURSES get 25 dollars per week and board. SCHOOL TEACHERS 100 dollars per month. GARDNERS 60 dollars per month and board. LABORERS 4 to 5 dollars per day. BRICKLAYERS 6 dollars per day. HOUSEKEEPERS 40 dollars per month. FARMERS 5 dollars per day. SHOEMAKERS 4 dollars per day. Men and Women COOKS 40 to 60 dollars per month and board. MINERS are making from 3 to 12 dollars per day. FEMALE SERVANTS 30 to 50 dollars per month and board. Washing 3 dollars per dozen. MASONS 6 dollars per day. CARPENTERS 5 dollars per day. ENGINEERS 100 dollars per month, and as the quartz Crushing Mills are getting into operation all through the country, Engineers are very scarce. BLACKSMITHS 90 and 100 dollars per month and board.

The above prices are copied from late papers printed in San Francisco, which can be seen at my office. Having views of some 30 Cities throughout the State of California, I shall be happy to see all who will call at the office of the Society, 28 JOY'S BUILDING, WASHINGTON ST., BOSTON, and examine them. Parties residing out of the City, by enclosing a stamp and sending to the office, will receive a circular giving all the particulars of the voyage.

As Agents are wanted in every town and city of the New England States, Postmasters or Merchants acting as such will be alowed a certain commission on every person they get to join the Company. Good reference required. For further particulars correspond or call at the

SOCIETY'S OFFICE,
28 Joy's Building, Washington St., Boston, Mass.

Propeller Job Press, 142 Washington Street, Boston.

Ann's mother had brought the rest of the family to America. They were of good, middle-class English stock and they proudly set up a carriage trade making upholstery and slipcovers.

When Mary Ann was 19 she met another English immigrant, John Ashworth Crabtree, a bookseller of Nassau Street. An easygoing, elegantly dressed man who spent more hours drinking than he did tending his bookstore, John Crabtree was nevertheless a charmer. Mary Ann married him in 1844.

The young woman continued to work in the family upholstery business, pausing only to have a child who died soon after birth. Lotta, her second child, was born on November 7, 1847.

Meanwhile, the discovery of gold in California in early 1848 was creating tales of unbelievable riches that went sweeping across the continent. John Crabtree was not untouched by the news. New York papers filled their pages with fabulous overnight success stories.

Horace Greeley of the *New York Tribune* wrote: "We are on the brink of an Age of Gold!"

The soundings were too much for the ambitious mind to ignore. John Crabtree held out until 1851 and then finally sold the bookstore, leaving for San Francisco with a promise to send for his wife and small daughter as soon as he was settled.

After some time passed, Mary Ann was summoned to California, and she and baby Lotta began the long and arduous trek westward. They chose to go by way of Panama, considered the easiest route of the time. Traveling first by boat, then by railroad,

and next by muleback through the thick, disease-infested jungles and torrid climates of South America, mother and daughter finally concluded the long journey on board the steam packet "Oregon."

Although husband John was not present to greet his family, Mary Ann soon set up housekeeping on Telegraph Hill. It was here that Lotta met and admired the colony of traveling actors. Among the troupe was the successful child actress Sue Robinson and a dozen other adult entertainers. Mary Ann must have recognized the potential of having a prodigy, for soon she enrolled Lotta in dancing classes.

Unsuccessful at discovering gold, John Crabtree reappeared, moving his wife and daughter to Grass Valley, high in the Sierras north of Sacramento. It was here that the famous Gold Hill Mine was founded, producing $1 million a year for nearly ninety-one years. As in other mining camps, tragedy, fire, and violence struck the town frequently, but its hidden treasures were worth the gamble.

Lotta's father never found gold. But fortunately for the family, his wife managed the funds by operating several boarding houses for miners. Here, too, the famous actress Lola Montez came and stayed with the family. And it was here that the aspiring dancing teacher, Bowers, polished the awakening talents of little Lotta.

Mary Ann became acquainted with another boarding house operator and former actress, Mrs. Harriet Robinson, who entertained at frequent bohemian circles of celebrities traveling the countryside. Lola Montez joined the group and immediately took

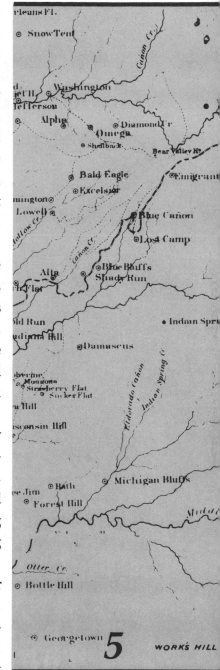

5   WORKS HILL

Lotta, in a posed publicity photograph

Lotta under her wing. In return, Lotta, impish and bright-eyed, adored the Countess, who would produce costumes from her trunks and let Lotta dance to the music from a German music box.

But it was a short stay in Grass Valley for the Crabtrees, as Mary Ann despairingly followed John from place to place before finally settling in La Porta, forty miles to the north. Once again she was cooking and making beds for the miners.

Sometime during this period the tempestuous Lola Montez, who had previously taught Lotta to ride horseback and dance the fandango and Highland fling, reappeared. Legend has it that Miss Montez wanted to take Lotta on a tour of Australia as her protégée. Mary Ann would not permit this, but all this attention from a celebrated star of the day merely confirmed Mary Ann's faith in her child's theatrical talent. Recognizing little Lotta's potential, her mother soon sought singing and dancing lessons from yet another teacher.

6 Matt Taylor had come west as a strolling musician, but in order to survive in this rapidly growing area, he had taken up the management of a local tavern. Next to this building he constructed a small log theater. During slack periods of the bar business, he taught dancing, singing, acting, and the like to whomever would pay.

Mary Ann was convinced of his abilities to teach her child, and soon Lotta became a delightful competitor to other traveling Fairy Stars. She quickly learned to dance the Irish jig, and wearing a pair of cobbled brogans, a miniature shillelagh and green breeches, a vest, and green satin top hat, she thrilled the Irish immigrant miners. The jig and the reel were followed by a group of tender ballads such as "How Can I Leave Thee?" Her performance was happily followed by a rain of quarters, gold nuggets, and Mexican dollars. The young entertainer collected these in a shoe and hastily put it all in the safe care of her mother.

Mother banks on daughter's talent

★ ★ ★ ★ ★ ★ ★

Mary Ann was an astute businesswoman as well as a stage mother, and she was quick to follow up on this unexpected new bounty. Leaving an unsettled husband in favor of taking her daughter on tour, she was later known to have told friends that "she was more interested in money than men." And for the remainder of her life, men were considered obstacles rather than the means of survival.

Her mother's fervent desire to see Lotta a great star did not hinder the child's future. Instead, being a thrifty woman, Mary Ann wisely managed the earnings, investing much of the gold and silver dollars (which she noted as "too heavy to carry") in property of the towns where the young performer

7

entertained. She carried a large leather grip later on, and much of the gifts and money were transferred to a steamer trunk for safekeeping. But investments continued all through Lotta's career.

While Lotta was still a child, another baby was born. And soon John Ashworth Crabtree, Jr., became part of the traveling company. Once again their father had disappeared on one of his many periodic excursions and it was time to take to the road, with the little family in Mary Ann's care. The magnificent pine-covered Sierras were truly beautiful to behold in summer. But for a small party on mules, they could be treacherous as well as scenic. It was usually quite warm during the sunlight hours, but at night the sky was blue-black, and a chill wind blew among the thick clumps of brush, which shadowed dark ravines.

Nevertheless, the traveling actors moved on. Led by strolling musician Matt Taylor beating his drum, the troupe would descend on the town.

Entering the small mining camps, some of which consisted of only tents or wooden shacks and saloons, Mary Ann would find a suitable place and engage it for several performances. Whether it was a barroom, a school, or a grocery store, it soon became a theatre with sawhorses and planks for a stage. The buildings were poorly built, and conditions were bad at best, with dirt floors, no heat, and blankets hung for stage curtains.

But the audience was enraptured with the elfin redhead and her whimsical twists and kicks. The lonely miners clapped and wept and hailed her as

Beat of drum announced touring minstrels

★ ★ ★ ★ ★ ★ ★

another Fairy Star. At the close of the performances, coins would be taken from worn money pouches and thrown, clattering, onto the sawhorse stage.

Occasionally, Lotta would become shy, and her mother would gently but firmly push her onto the stage. But she soon overcame this, and once she was the center attraction, Lotta turned professional. The family would travel all summer long, Lotta dancing bashfully and boldly by turns, kicking her feet and singing with a growing charm. Mary Ann was the one to impose discipline and to offer encouragement when needed, but Lotta was becoming the star.

As time went on, Mary Ann fashioned a stove-pipe hat with no top. With this the child gathered the coins, watching with puzzled amusement as they rattled back onto the floor boards. The crowds of miners loved this innocent scene and soon it became part of the act. Mary Ann recognized also that it was the character songs that Lotta did best and the audiences enjoyed most. Trouping across the northern California counties, Lotta was blackface, Irish, or patriotic, depending on the mood. Soon she became the pet of the miners, and she would be carried off stage on a miner's shoulders.

As the child's repertoire of songs grew, Mary Ann found that one of the favorites was Lotta's impersonation of Topsy from Harriet Beecher Stowe's *Uncle Tom's Cabin*. "It's so wicked," she would exclaim over and over with a mixture of deviltry and innocence in her voice. The routine became so popular that it remained part of her act through most of her long career.

In the winter the family returned to San Francisco for more voice and piano lessons for Lotta. Then in the spring, they boarded a stagecoach and headed into the Sacramento Valley. Mary Ann did impersonations of various celebrities while her daughter was doing a remarkable soft-shoe number, gleaned earlier from a minstrel player. They sold Taylor's *Gold Digger's Song Book* and sometimes earned as much as $400 a night. Often the take depended on the previous day's work for the miners: if luck had been good, the coins dancing on the stage were numerous; if luck had been poor, money was scarce. But Lotta continued to shuffle, sing ballads of the day, and mimic other actors. Never at a loss for material, Lotta and her mother were discovering a hungry world eager to be entertained.

When Lotta was 10 years old, her father, who had returned home, tried to persuade the owner of Maguire's Opera House in San Francisco to hire his young daughter. When he declined to do so, Crabtree fired his pistol, grazing the surprised Tom Maguire, who went away unscathed and unperturbed. Two years later, Lotta *was* hired to perform at Maguire's Opera House, the previous incident seemingly forgotten. She was the youngest member of the cast in those days but was a strong contender for success. With Mary Ann's boundless confidence, a theatrical future seemed near at hand.

The Crabtree family was close-knit despite the father's wanderings, and now, with two brothers shipped off to school in Europe, they were all proud of the sister who was making it possible.

Performers in those days were versatile, engaging in comedy skits and serious drama, singing and dancing, and playing several instruments. Their performances were well received in small theatres and melodeons. True, their efforts were geared for a solidly masculine audience, but Mary Ann was always present, demanding that her daughter be respected and treated as a young lady of class.

By the late 1850s Lotta was known as "La Petit Lotta, the Celebrated Danseuse and Vocalist" and as "Miss Lotta, the San Francisco Favorite." She was a budding star.

The discovery of fantastic wealth in the Comstock Lode in 1859 opened up another location for traveling entertainers. Tom Maguire had built another theatre in the booming Nevada town, and Lotta and Mary Ann soon ventured eastward. The miners were rough and bawdy but loved all musical entertainment. However, the Civil War was just beginning, so performers had to slant their acts in the direction of the audiences' sympathies or be faced with leaving town in a hurry. It's said that Lotta and her mother made such a mistake in one theatre. After the curtain fell to a silent audience, they quickly retreated to San Francisco.

Actors well received in mining camps

★ ★ ★ ★ ★ ★ ★

Undaunted, Lotta played in the American Theatre for fire benefits, and in amusement parks of northern California. About this time, Lotta met the famous actress, Adah Isaacs Menken, who helped her perfect her theatrical talents. Lotta also learned to smoke long black cigars from this flamboyant woman. Little did she know that later in life this would become a trademark of sorts.

During the California years Lotta Crabtree had

11

many successes, and her reputation as a fine performer was growing. But her mother felt she should expand to greater fields, so at 16 years of age, Lotta and Mary Ann set out for New York City—but not before a grand farewell benefit at Maguire's Opera House was held, netting Lotta $1500. With this and the previous earnings still intact, thanks to Mary Ann, the family headed for the East Coast, again by way of Panama.

The elegant theatres of New York and their audiences, however, were used to more sophisticated entertainment, and despite Lotta's efforts, her first venture into the eastern city failed. Pulling up stakes, they went on to Chicago, where crowds were more friendly, and as they traveled through Pennsylvania and Ohio, Lotta's confidence soon returned.

Playing as many as six roles in a single play, the tiny redhead switched easily from a character of saucy impertinence to one overflowing with sentimentality. Topsy was always a success, but there were also "The Captain with His Whiskers Gave a Sly Wink at Me," and patriotic numbers, "Rally Round the Flag Boys," and "Dear Mother, I'll Come Home Again." She went easily from soldier's uniform to Indian paint and concluded the show in Irish garb, invariably with her clogs thundering to banjo music. Lotta burlesqued the famous Jenny Lind and Lola Montez. Her dances included hornpipes, Scottish flings, shuffles, and polkas. Audiences responded enthusiastically; their approval of

☞ *The Drummer Boy, a miner favorite*

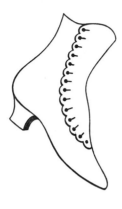

the young actress was overwhelming. Yet it was invariably the parody, the single kick, a dozen daring antics, and her final bounce off the stage, which left one shapely ankle peeking out from under the curtain, that brought the audience to their feet. Lotta was a performer, and she knew how to excite her fans.

Rave reviews followed her now wherever she performed. One in Boston called her "a burst of fresh air from the west," while other newspapers were equally enthusiastic.

Her repertoire increased as the years rolled by, and Lotta participated in legitimate plays as well as comic routines. She earned as much as $10,000 for several weeks' run in the eastern houses, and enjoyed the after-hours parties and flirtations that accompanied such success.

The country in the 1860s was soon caught up in the Lotta Polka and the Lotta Gallop, two popular dance crazes that swept the larger cities.

With Mary Ann minding the business interests and Lotta making more and more money, her father and other relatives soon found ways to spend her increasing earnings. The family had always stood together, and despite an easy flow of funds, later losses, and poor ventures, they remained closely knit. One exception was Lotta's father, who was later pensioned off to England. Ironically, he told his English relatives he had "made it" in the California gold fields.

Lotta had hundreds of admirers and young men eager to become friendlier. Mary Ann, however, was not about to have her venture into some unfortunate liaison, and so discouraged any close relationships. Lotta had come to depend on her mother not only as a manager, but also as an advisor. Perhaps it was for this reason that she never married.

Among her close companions was J. Bolton Hulme, scion of a wealthy Philadelphia family. They became close friends, but the newspapers made more of their relationship. Unfortunately, he liked to drink and gamble, using Lotta's money. But she seems to have been sincerely in love with him, and when he died suddenly a few years later, reporters said "something in Lotta had died with him."

She continued to receive gifts of gold watches, lockets, jewels of all kinds and shapes, and various other keepsakes. She met the Grand Duke Alexis of Russia during an engagement in New Orleans. He was making a celebrated visit to the United States. He chose to visit the theatre and was captivated by tiny Lotta and her charming performance. Afterwards, the seven-foot-tall Duke invited her aboard his ship. He was so enthralled with her that a week later she was presented with a bracelet of dazzling diamonds, opals, and pearls.

Lotta received many other honors as well and was proud of medals and awards presented to her from baseball clubs, bellboys, and newspaper boys. Playing a stage urchin, clothed as a homeless newspaper boy, she captivated this group, and soon she had a national following.

She and Mary Ann traveled abroad, sometimes with brother Jack and younger brother John Jr. Lotta spent time studying French as well as visiting art

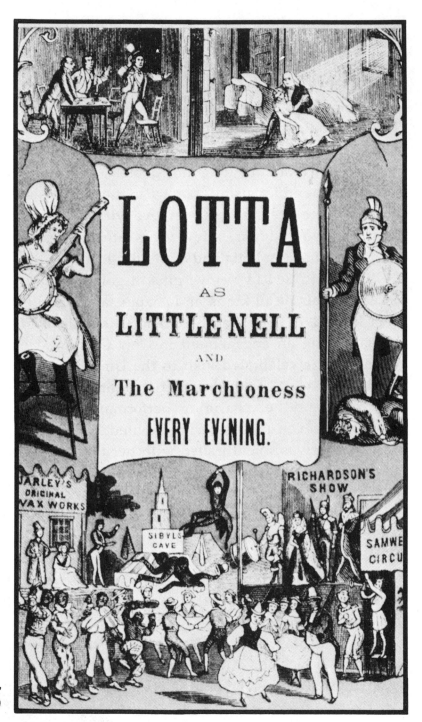

16

galleries. It was during one of these European visits that she took up painting, a hobby she pursued for the rest of her life.

As her success mounted, she began to perform in more and more charity benefits, gaining the enduring gratitude of fire companies. Her interest changed to doing plays such as Frederic Marsden's "Musette" and "Little Bright Eyes." Playwrights wrote plays for her, and "Zip," "Little Nell," and "Firefly" became personal favorites. Yet it seems that the audiences liked the Cinderella plays most. Lotta found the longer plays difficult to memorize quickly and took to improvising, much to the dismay of the cast. The audiences, however, loved this.

After Bolt Hulme's death, Lotta was frequently entertained by Francis L. Wellman, the son of a proud Boston family. He never married her. Newspaper gossip columnists claimed this was because his father did not want him married to an actress. However, they remained lasting friends.

In 1875 Lotta commissioned a Philadelphia company to cast a large statue for her. It was to be a symbolic gesture toward the city of San Francisco and their love for her. Costing $10,000, the giant 30-foot "Watering Spot", as it was called, was shipped west in sections and erected at the intersections of Geary, Market, and Kearny Streets. A magnificent piece of work, its fluted shaft is decorated with the heads of griffins, bears, and seals and is surrounded by wrought-iron lilies. These, in turn, support a large lantern crowned with streams bearing three groups of golden balls. The people loved it. Four years later Lotta came west for its dedication.

While she was in San Francisco she met and fell in love with Henry E. Abbey. The young impresario, though married, also appears to have been in love with the ageless performer. Lotta backed him in the purchase of the Park Theatre in New York and their association endured. When his wife died, however, he suddenly married actress Florence Gerard. Columnists wrote once again that the shattered affair "broke Lotta's heart." This seems untrue. Lotta was known to be fickle and to enjoy the company of many men. Also, she no doubt found fulfillment in being a star, in always being center stage. The thought of having to share this with another, or at best pretending she was not always number one, may have made it easier to remain unmarried.

Mary Ann continued to manage her daughter's affairs, booking plays, organizing traveling troupes of actors, and seeking out locations. Always a shrewd businesswoman, she often demanded 70 percent of the take rather than the normal 60 percent, and always requested top billing for Lotta.

There were, however, some poor investments along the way, much to the disappointment of Lotta's mother. She invested in a cotton firm and a gold mine and backed other endeavors that went broke. But Lotta's stage appearances continued to bring in great rewards, so the family was never in want. If they wished to go abroad, give someone money, or build a home for a relative, they did.

Lotta Crabtree retired from the theatre at the age

Lotta, ready for a character role

General Clarence R. Edwards, Bostonian,
professional soldier, friend and advisor to Lotta

of 45, and she and her mother retreated to their
"summer cottage," a 17-room estate in northern New
Jersey. Attol (Lotta spelled backwards) Tryst still
stands today. Lotta spent her days painting and
enjoying those thinly rolled black cigars. It was this
habit that kept her from becoming a member of the
socially prominent group, Sorosis. Founded by
literary-minded women in New York City, it later
became the General Federation of Women's Clubs.

When Lotta's mother died in 1905, something
inside Lotta died also. For the first time she began to
show her real age. Lotta tried visiting Europe again
but came home suddenly, still saddened by Mary
Ann's death.

"What I am, what I have been, and what I was, I
owe entirely to her. . . . My mother was the most

20

wonderful woman that ever lived, and I want the world to know it." She made these remarks at "Lotta Crabtree Day" in the fall of 1915 in San Francisco. The occasion was the Panama–Pacific Exposition, and the townspeople had turned out to remember their own Fairy Star.

To further show her love for Mary Ann, Lotta had a stained-glass window crafted in her honor. The tribute remains today, part of the splendor of St. Stephen's Church in Chicago.

Lotta bought the Brewster Hotel in New York City and remained there until her death, catering to theatre people. When she was late into her 70s, she met General Clarence R. Edwards, a Bostonian who was a professional soldier. They spent hours together, discussing horses and her will. Lotta had once owned a stable of trotters, and this provided a common ground for conversation. The aging actress also wished to leave $100,000 to aid in the rehabilitation of soldiers returning from World War I. Edwards persuaded her to leave $2 million. They remained friends until her death in 1924 at the age of 77. She was buried quietly in Woodlawn Cemetery in New York City, next to her mother.

She left an estate estimated at $4 million. Despite the fact that she wanted the money to go to "dumb animals" and "doughboys of World War I," a long and colorful court battle over rightful heirs followed. Her will was eventually settled; a trust was established for humane and educational purposes for the young. But while the court battle was still being waged, the newspapers once again brought to life the exciting and illustrious career of Lotta Crabtree.

Leaves estate valued at $4 million

★ ★ ★ ★ ★ ★ ★

21

CHARLIE PARKHURST

A LIFETIME OF DISGUISE

22

He was sitting straight and riding easy atop the Wells Fargo stagecoach, the reins grasped between his gloved fingers, sharing a bottle with his partner, Ed Maguire. There seemed nothing remarkable about him; he was just another stage driver bent on making his run. It was the spring of '59 and I was a kid, with long braids the color of dried wheat batting at my ears and getting in the way of sitting down. Me and Ma and Baby John were coming west from Pittsburgh to join Pa, who had come to California to seek his fortune in gold. This was the last leg of our long, hard journey. We capped the Sierras and began our hazardous ride down the mountains to Placerville. I'd been sick for the last couple of hours and was just praying we'd get to a watering station soon.

But it was Charlie Parkhurst that really kept my mind busy. He was up there on top of the world, the warm sun beating down on his rugged face, which barely showed beneath the wide brim of a muddy tan hat. A knotted handkerchief was tied around his neck, and he wore leather pants and scuffed boots with high heels that made him walk like a cowboy and not like anything I'd seen back home. All trace of newness was long since gone from his clothes. The dust of travel was beaten into them. They were stained and mended around the deep pockets. Yet a kind of Wild West adventure surrounded him, and I couldn't keep from wondering about his curious face.

23

Ma must have sensed what I was thinking, for she shook her head scoldingly. "Amy, remember your manners. He can't help wearing a black patch over his eye. Probably lost it fighting off some wild savages."

I guess she was probably right. At least it was an interesting thought, making him taller in my eyes. Ma had always been scared of Indians. I don't know why; we'd never seen any in Pittsburgh. Oh, maybe *she* had, once. But I hadn't, least of all the scalping kind. What worried me was meeting up with one of those dangerous outlaws haunting the trails that we'd heard so much about. Besides, guns—even Pa's—made my ears ring.

"Amy," Ma said again, "looks like we're coming to a stop. See that cluster of frame buildings up ahead?"

She must have had real good eyes, for it was hard to see anything out the window, except the clouds of choking yellow dust billowing up. Occasionally, I could see the peaks of the tall mountains on either side. A stop and a cup of cold water sure would be welcome.

I was staring out the window again, my braids flying over my shoulders, when Charlie drew in the reins of the tired horse team, yelling at several men who came out of the wood cabin. Here we would take on mail, water, and a change of horses.

"Hey, Charlie!" an unshaven, scruffy-clothed man shouted. "Good to see you. Got another load of them city folks with you?"

One-eyed Charlie swung down from the wagon seat, stamping his feet and slapping dust from his clothes. His glance hit me, dismissed me, and went back to the men. Three others sat on the covered porch, playing cards and drinking.

"We ain't got much time," he shouted. "Want to make it down the mountain before dark."

"Got time for a beer, ain't you?"

"Sure," he grinned, pushing back his hat and ambling up the wooden steps.

The sudden halting motion of the coach must have caused my stomach to flop over again. Embarrassed, I ran quickly to the bushes and began to retch. Ma was getting out of the stage, carrying the baby and casting a suspicious eye on the bearded cowboy who helped her. Maguire, the other driver, had gotten down with the mail bag and was staggering into the store.

"We'll get you some water, Amy," Ma said. "Just go lay down on the grass for a minute."

I didn't reply, but Baby John woke up and started crying loudly. Ma went back to feed him.

I lay down in one of the taller clumps of grass, letting my bare hands and face feel the cool blades. In the stillness the voices carried easily. Charlie had joined the group of men on the porch and was shooting dice for a beer. I could smell the familiar cigar smoke drifting over my head. Far above me in the crystalline sky, two huge black birds circled. Probably waiting for me to die so they could have a good meal, I thought. It wouldn't be long the way I was feeling. All around me were towering mountains, groves of thick pine trees outlining their crest. Patches of dried grass ran alongside the wagon trail, with large boulders sticking up almost everywhere.

Heading down the trail

This gold country was sure different from the plains we had crossed earlier, and I guessed it would probably be a nice place to live. But right now the ground was hard, the scented air unbearable, and my stomach just wouldn't stop hurting.

I don't remember how much time passed before I opened my eyes, but I looked into the one kindly brown eye of Charlie Parkhurst.

"Here, girl," he said gently, his whiskey breath beating down on me. "Try this. It'll help your ailing."

"What's in the cup?" I asked cautiously.

"Just a little sarsaparilla to settle your stomach."

"But I shouldn't."

Charlie forced the cup into my hands. Ma would have been furious if she'd seen me drinking it. Her Bible teaching didn't allow this kind of drink, but it couldn't have made me feel worse than I was already feeling. I swallowed the thick brown liquid, feeling it tingle as it went down my throat.

Charlie took the metal cup, patted my forehead, and smiled. "Now just lay still till we're ready to leave. You'll be feelin' better soon." I tried to smile back, but it wasn't easy.

I lay in the grass for a long time, listening to Baby John crying. Ma was talking to someone, and then another man called out to Charlie.

"Have a good trip," he said. "And keep an eye out for that bandit, Sugarfoot. He's been raising hell with some of the other stage drivers."

"We ain't carrying much worth holding us up for," Charlie sounded reassuring. "Just them three passengers, their belongings, and some mail and currency."

"Well, you never know about outlaws. Just keep an eye open."

"Sure will. Hey, Maguire," Charlie shouted back, "Come on. Want to make it down the mountain before dark."

Maguire stumbled back out the door and down the steps and dragged his fat belly onto the top of the stage. Charlie came over and got me up, helping me back to the coach. Ma was inside fussing with Baby John, who must have been feeling about as poorly as I was, for he was still crying. But Ma was smiling like an angel, her brown hair falling loose from under her bonnet. Ma had the most beautiful green eyes I had ever seen, but right now they looked tired and discouraged. She was probably wondering if we were ever going to see Pa again. It had been a long trip—it seemed like months—and not an easy journey. We had come as far as the railroad would go and then came the rest of the way by stagecoach.

Charlie gave me a boost inside, pulling one of my braids and slapping my rear. "Not much farther, girl," he said. "Just keep up your spirits."

"Yeah," I said. "And thanks for the drink. It helped my pains considerably."

I crawled onto the seat next to Ma and the baby, brushing strands of hair off my forehead. Ma pushed my muslin skirts down and went back to tending the baby.

Soon the big, wooden wheels were rolling again, bouncing and bumping over the rocky dirt trail that led to Placerville. I watched the sun dip behind a hill and then reappear suddenly as we came around a bend, the stage half tipping over as it flew over the ground. Charlie was up in the seat, yelling and cracking his long whip in the air, getting as much speed out of our fresh horses as was humanly possible.

"Yo!" he shouted. The whip was snapping, and the yellow dust was blowing around the window.

It was turning cold now, and I looked about the cluttered stage for the woolen shawl Grandmother Thompson had made for me before we left home. "Wear it, child," she had said, knowing she'd prob-

☆ ☆ ☆ ☆ ☆ ☆ ☆

Yo, *he shouted,*

the whip

snapping

ably never see us again. "Keep warm on those cold California nights." Then I didn't think California would ever be cold. But I had been wrong. The Sierra Nevadas turned icy when the sun went down.

I choked on the endless dust swirling about our stage. Suddenly a chill ran down my spine clear to my toes. Through the haze, I saw three masked bandits coming down the hillside. Their legs dug deeply into their horses' sides and they were waving guns and shouting at us to stop.

"Pull up," the leader ordered, letting go with several blasts of his gun over our stage.

My ears rang and my eyes must have been the size of silver dollars as I watched them force us to a halt. I wondered what Charlie was doing now, but I couldn't move. My legs were locked in place.

When the dust had settled down, I gained enough courage to look out again. Ma was squeezing my shoulder, sure the end had come. "Be still, Amy," she gasped, "Be still."

Baby John must not have heard her, for he was letting go with all he had, crying and kicking up a storm. I didn't know how the outlaws would take to his demands.

"Pull her in," the outlaw shouted while the other two men jumped down from their horses. They were carrying the longest-barrel guns I had ever seen, and their eyes, peeking out above the handkerchiefs, looked as fierce as any wild savage's.

"Toss down the rifles," he yelled at Charlie and Maguire, "then get that money chest out, and tell the people inside to get out."

29

Charlie and Maguire climbed down from their seats, opening the door to the stage and helping me and Ma out. I wished that Baby John would stop crying.

"Over to one side," yelled the leader, waving his gun. He was dirty and terrible and mean as anything I had ever seen.

Charlie pulled the strongbox down off the stage, and let it drop to the ground right in front of my toes. I looked down at it just as a bullet went smashing into the lock, causing it to shatter against my skirts. I let out a yell, then quickly covered my mouth with my hands.

"Sugarfoot won't harm kids, not if they mind themselves," the man on the horse called. "Now, kid, since you're the closest, take off that broken lock and open up the box."

I looked up at Charlie for direction, but he made no move. His hands were over his head, his one good eye shadowed by the brim of his hat. My hero didn't look so brave and strong any more.

Bending down, I worked at the lock, finally getting it loose and pulling it off. Then I pushed up the heavy lid. It was full all right, packed with bills marked in different denominations and all neatly tied. There was, however, no gold. I straightened up and turned once more to stare into the wicked eyes of Sugarfoot. He had gotten off his horse and was moving steadily toward me and the box.

"So," he said, "Got some of the president's own. Look here, boys. What do you make of this?"

But the boys were busy taking Ma's gold locket

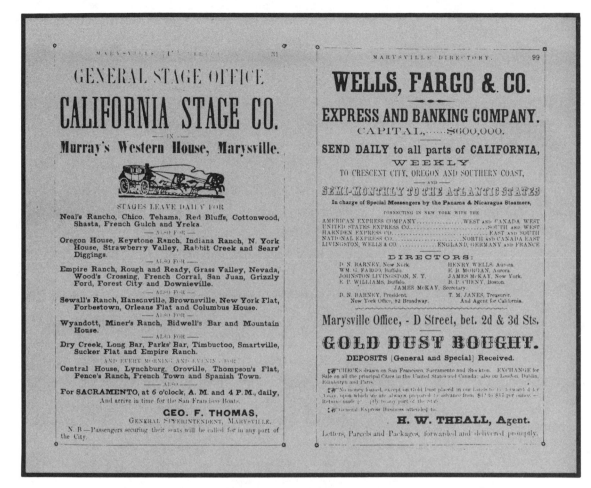

Posters of the day

with the opal setting that Pa had given her, and a shiny watch that Maguire had tried to hide in the pocket of his pants.

"Come on," Sugarfoot snapped, "We haven't got all day. Grab that box and let's get going."

I'm not sure just what happened next, but I recall hearing gunshots and seeing two men fall face down into the dirt. Charlie had grabbed a gun that he kept

31

hidden in the stagecoach and had moved swiftly into action. He pushed me to the ground, shooting as his body twisted away, bringing Sugarfoot to the ground also. The other outlaws had run for their horses. But Charlie was a dead shot, and before I could catch my breath it was all over. Maguire was moaning, trying to lift up his body on one elbow and holding his other arm. One of Sugarfoot's men managed to get up on his horse.

"He's getting away!" I shouted.

But Charlie said nothing and went over to Maguire. The notorious Sugarfoot lay face down in the dirt next to him. His body was still.

"You okay, Ed?" Charlie asked, bending over his friend and taking off the scarf around his neck. He stuck the gun into the belt of his pants and then looked at Maguire's arm. I guess that with all the booze Maguire had consumed, he wasn't feeling much pain. At least he wasn't moaning that bad. He just looked up at Charlie and cursed the outlaws who had laid him low.

Charlie helped him up, lifting him inside the stagecoach.

"He'd better ride back there with you, ma'am," he said to Ma. "Think you can keep the wound from bleeding too bad?"

Only a few seconds ago Ma had looked like she had seen the Great Beyond, but being a strong woman despite her diminutive size, she immediately grasped the situation. Laying Baby John on the seat (which was about time, since he just wasn't going to stop crying even when Ma held him), she helped Maguire get comfortable. Charlie took me by the arm.

"Maybe your stomach would feel better if you rode in the open with me. Come on, your Ma has got her hands full. Get up there on the seat. We ain't got much farther to go, anyway."

Trying to hide my pleasure, I obediently climbed up to the top of the stage, tucking my muslin skirts underneath my legs and pushing my braids back off my shoulders. Charlie slammed the stage doors, locking Ma and Maguire and Baby John inside. Tossing the rifle up on the seat next to me, he jumped up, his hands closing about the reins.

The whip cracked in the chill air and his voice echoed through the canyons. Digging into the soft dirt, the stage wheels spun and then rolled forward. The weight of the coach made us race down the mountain.

I held on as best I could, watching Charlie skillfully maneuver the stage around a jagged boulder that had tumbled down the hillside and then down a long, winding road that made a hairpin curve into a pretty green valley far below. Suddenly we were rolling close to a sharp ledge. Giant pines shot up one side of the trail, but on the other side I saw nothing but the deepening shadows below. I thought we were dangerously close to the edge, but Charlie didn't slow the pace of the animals. Instead, he whipped at the air and yelled louder at the team. Our wheels turned faster than ever. I nearly swallowed my tongue, staring down from the top of the stagecoach into the dark hole running past our

Charlie handles the reins with skill and courage

wheels. But I didn't say a word; I just pulled my shawl closer about me. Charlie was in complete control of his coach, and besides, as he said, "We had valuable time to make up."

When he did see the flickering lights of the town ahead, the sun had slipped behind the mountains and the raw night air was already biting at my cheeks. Charlie was quiet, chewing some tobacco and whistling a little tune. I had forgotten my stomach.

Finally Charlie looked over at me, smiling just like Pa would have. "Well, you got something to tell the kids about now," he said, putting his arm around my shoulders. "You're a brave little girl. That's what this country needs to make it grow."

I never forgot that long journey west to California, and neither did I forget ol' one-eyed Charlie. I had never seen anything quite like him, and I guess I never shall again. Of course, Charlie became a real hero among the other stage drivers after killing Sugarfoot and saving his passengers and the government currency.

Some years later, in January 1880, when I was a mother with growing children, an article in the *San Franciso Call* caught my eye and sent my heart skidding back into time. According to the newspaper account, declining health and age had forced Charlie Parkhurst to retire ten years ago. He had spent the rest of his life as a recluse in Aptos, California. When he died a few days ago, his body was taken to the mortuary to be prepared for its final resting place. To the utter surprise of the local mortician, Charlie turned out to be a woman.

"She had fooled everyone for the better part of fifty years. The reasons for her disguise and her way of life are not known to us. We can only speculate on her reasons."

She achieved distinction in a physical occupation that called for nerve, courage, endurance, and coolness—qualities arrogantly claimed to be exclusively masculine. What made the story even more interesting was this: "It was a recorded fact that he registered and voted in the Santa Cruz County election in 1868. And by so doing became the first woman ever to cast a ballot in the United States."

ELANOR DUMONT

MADAM MOUSTACHE

Elanor Dumont sat alone in the small frame cabin outside Bodie, California. Her black hair was streaked with grey; her once pretty brown eyes merely reflected a lifetime of gambling, wild Gold Rush adventures, and questionable morals. She'd known men of instant wealth and others who had staked no claims. One no-good, thieving scamp married her and then later ran off with all her savings. It was not the thought of him that hurt so much, but rather the heavy memories of an illustrious life compared with what she was now, at 45 years of age.

"Look at yourself," she said aloud, catching sight of the pale, wrinkled face in a broken mirror in the deserted cabin. "Faded, ugly Madam Moustache. God!" she exclaimed. "How could I have let anyone call me that, even in jest. So a little hair grew on my upper lip. Other women had that, too. The men used to think it masculine and exciting for a beautiful woman to have hair on her body. But not now. Now that I'm old."

The door swung silently open. A gust of summer air flicked bits of dried grass and leaves across the floor, sending them scurrying up against her worn taffeta skirts. Elanor didn't notice the dirt. Instead her gaze wandered past the opening down the long desolate trail skirted with sagebrush and rock. Several miles away lay the town of Bodie, known as the most lawless, wildest, and toughest mining camp in the Far West. At its zenith it had nearly 10,000 gold-

37

frenzied inhabitants: miners, gamblers, business-men, prostitutes, land speculators. All sought one thing—gold—and were forever trying to take it away from those who dug it from the earth. So wicked and rip-roaring was the town that someone was prompted to write to a northern newspaper, "Good-bye God! I'm going to Bodie."

But Madam Moustache couldn't handle it any longer. Alone and deserted, she was worn out at mid-life. A squirrel ran past the door, pausing to poke its head under an opening in the dilapidated structure. He caught her eye. "Young and full of adventure," she thought, recalling another scene long ago.

It was Nevada City, California in the year 1854. A beautiful, 20-year-old brunette had stepped off the Concord stage. Her laughing French eyes and kindly smile attracted all those who stood nearby. They in turn smiled back.

"Welcome to the county seat and the third largest city in California," a dusty miner yelled, swinging his muddy felt hat across the ground in a gesture of gallantry. "What's a pretty lady like you coming to a wild town like this for?"

Elanor nodded sweetly, picking up the hem of her woolen skirts.

A constant noise of horses and people shouting enthusiastically echoed through this gold-mining town built on hilly terrain. New buildings with touches of Victorian gingerbread and others built merely of canvas and wood had sprung up over-night. Between 15,000 and 35,000 miners and others huddled along the creeks and clung to hillsides.

Seventy-nine saloons and the first theatre in the Sierras dotted the bustling streets.

The sky was a brilliant blue, and the air warm and inviting. Two more dirty but beaming cowboys jumped forward to help Elanor with her luggage. She looked like a sophisticated eastern schoolgirl, perhaps the pure daughter of a preacher. Other young men paused to stare, willing to do most anything just for a smile from the newly arrived enchantress.

Elanor was a pretty young woman, with flashing eyes and a fine figure. She was wearing a stylish blue wool suit with long skirts, which revealed her ivory-buttoned shoes and a pair of shapely ankles. A flopping sapphire hat with matching ribbons and white plumage adorned her head. In a town with few single women, her charms were rapidly announced.

Elanor found a clean hotel, and after several days of checking the potential of the unbelievably rich little town, she decided on a likely spot to set up business. To the horror of the respectable townsfolk who hoped for added stability, the pretty young woman, obviously cultivated with a fine upbringing, opened a gambling parlor on Broad Street.

Unbothered by town gossip, for she had experienced the same public opinion in the Colorado mining camps she had just left, Elanor set up shop. Soon her friendliness and unselfishness made her a favorite among all the folks of Nevada City. It was noted by early researchers that her personal charm was so great that everyone soon forgave her—even the losers. And there were many of those. Elanor was an excellent card player, and personally dealt the game

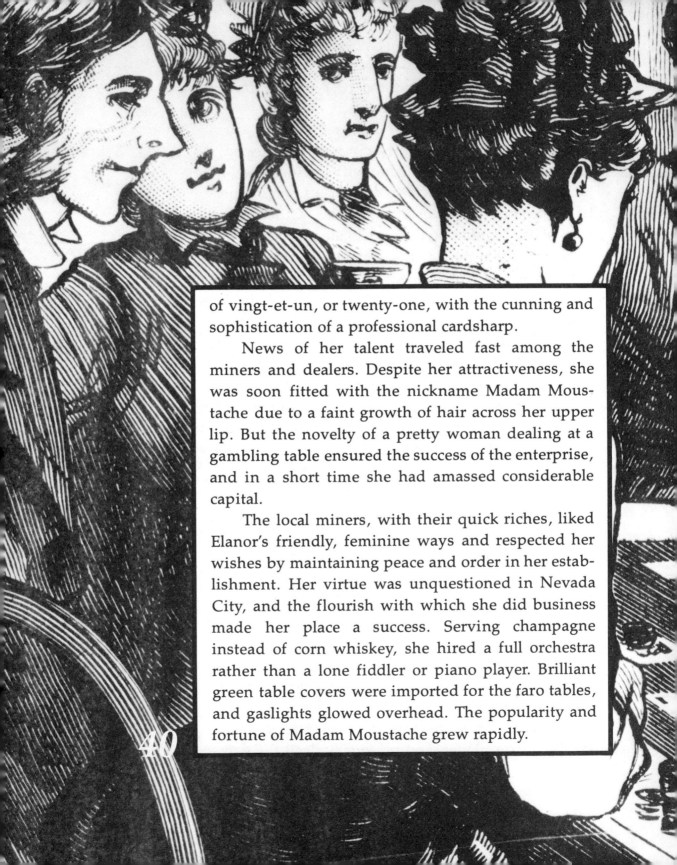

of vingt-et-un, or twenty-one, with the cunning and sophistication of a professional cardsharp.

News of her talent traveled fast among the miners and dealers. Despite her attractiveness, she was soon fitted with the nickname Madam Moustache due to a faint growth of hair across her upper lip. But the novelty of a pretty woman dealing at a gambling table ensured the success of the enterprise, and in a short time she had amassed considerable capital.

The local miners, with their quick riches, liked Elanor's friendly, feminine ways and respected her wishes by maintaining peace and order in her establishment. Her virtue was unquestioned in Nevada City, and the flourish with which she did business made her place a success. Serving champagne instead of corn whiskey, she hired a full orchestra rather than a lone fiddler or piano player. Brilliant green table covers were imported for the faro tables, and gaslights glowed overhead. The popularity and fortune of Madam Moustache grew rapidly.

As business prospered in the gold-hungry atmosphere of the mining town, Elanor took on a partner, David Tobin, a professional gambler. Together they opened a larger and more elaborate establishment, he taking charge of the bigger games and handling keno and faro. He also must have been helpful in handling the robust and often violent customers. Fights and killings were an everyday occurrence in the California mining camps, and they often resulted in short trials and quick hangings. Arguments arose rapidly after too much whiskey and high-stake gambling. Yet the frenzied pace increased.

Despite the violent overtones of masculine activities, Elanor exercised considerable influence over her rough clientele. It is said that once the room in which she conducted her games had been filled with a noisy and quarrelsome drunken group, flourishing revolvers and bound for a free-for-all. Bartenders and others had attempted to quell the riot, but without much success. Suddenly Madam Dumont quietly approached the noisiest of the crowd. Laughingly, she scolded him and the rest for their ungallant conduct, and succeeded in clearing the room and averting the threatened fight.

The gambling establishment was kept open day and night, and Elanor was a great favorite, paying all losses with a bright smile, and raking in all gains with the stoic indifference of a true gambler. At this point in her life, Madam Moustache commanded not only much admiration, but also the respect of the unruly '49ers.

42

She and Tobin continued their partnership for

over a year until he left for New York. In 1865 he died, leaving a large fortune.

Unlike other mining camps, Nevada City was destined to become a permanent town, complete with law and order and fine residents. The fact that it was the county seat helped, as did the prosperity of its close neighbor, Grass Valley.

Then came the news from the assay office that ore from the Comstock Lode in Nevada was fantastically rich. By 1859 the miners were leaving as fast as they had come ten years before. Eyeing the new discoveries in terms of her own business, Elanor wandered from camp to camp along the Mother Lode, never remaining long in one place. Yet she was always a favorite visitor. Miners often said that it was more of a satisfaction to lose money to her than to win from anyone else. She was always generous to the unfortunate and ready to stake a luckless miner. By the 1870s she was a living legend throughout the west.

Elanor continued to travel to wherever she heard miners were "striking it rich." For she, too, had to depend on gold discoveries for her livelihood. Across the dusty, hazardous overland trails she ventured, topping the majestic Sierra Nevada mountains, undaunted by freezing weather or roving highwaymen. Robbing the miners of their newly-found gold was a common practice in those days, just as was gambling, brawling, and killing. But Elanor had little fear.

Once, after winning a small purse, she was set upon by two unruly footpads. It was late, but miners were still drinking and quarreling inside the nearby saloons. Elanor was making her way down the dark road toward her home when the two men suddenly jumped out of hiding, demanding her house winnings.

"I'll do no such thing," she said, clutching her woolen shawl about her thin shoulders.

Holding guns on her, their breath smelling of corn whiskey, the assailants ordered, "Give us the money or you'll be a sorry woman."

Elanor nodded. With the grace and skill of a well-schooled woman, she deftly reached into her taffeta skirts. But instead of bringing forth the money, she produced a small derringer and instantly killed one of them. His partner fled.

Needless to say, her reputation soared to even greater heights.

One researcher notes that Elanor was chiefly admired for her "rustling" qualities. In Boise City, Idaho, she succeeded in raising a stake and opening her own bank at a time when every other gambler in town was stranded for lack of funds.

For the next several years she maintained an establishment in Bannock, Montana, and here she expanded her activities. Games of chance and a saloon were situated on the first floor; prostitution was the second-floor business. One of her upstairs "boarders" was a 15-year-old named Martha Jane Canary, alias Calamity Jane.

But Elanor appeared not to have enduring ties, and she moved on to San Francisco. According to historians there, "She attempted to queen it in the

San Francisco demimonde as proprietress of an establishment for French women, only gambling was distinctly not one of the amusements. . . ."

She lived in a glitter of stylish furnishings and dressed in the latest fashions, all provided by numerous wealthy gentlemen friends. But ill luck and age forced Madam Moustache to succumb to the common fate of "fast" women of her time: she became a prostitute herself. Having once earned her living entirely by using wit and skill, she must have had some regrets about her current line of work.

Whatever her reasons, Elanor once again set out to seek her fortune in the California and Nevada mining camps. This time, however, she was not as lucky—and certainly not as young and beautiful.

Perhaps tired of the fast-paced life and its sudden violence, she decided to get married. Having saved several thousand dollars, she decided to share it with the man she loved. She purchased a farm in eastern Nevada, turning over her real estate and earnings to her husband. It had been her often-expressed dream to settle in the country and spend her remaining years in peace and quiet.

Not much was known of her husband other than that he was a small-time promoter who liked to gamble and play cards. However, he proved to be a worthless scamp, and after squandering all her savings, he deserted Madam Moustache, leaving her to resume the only kind of life that would allow her to survive. Any one of her past acquaintances would have willingly brought him back to face the consequences, but Elanor chose to let him go. Driven by

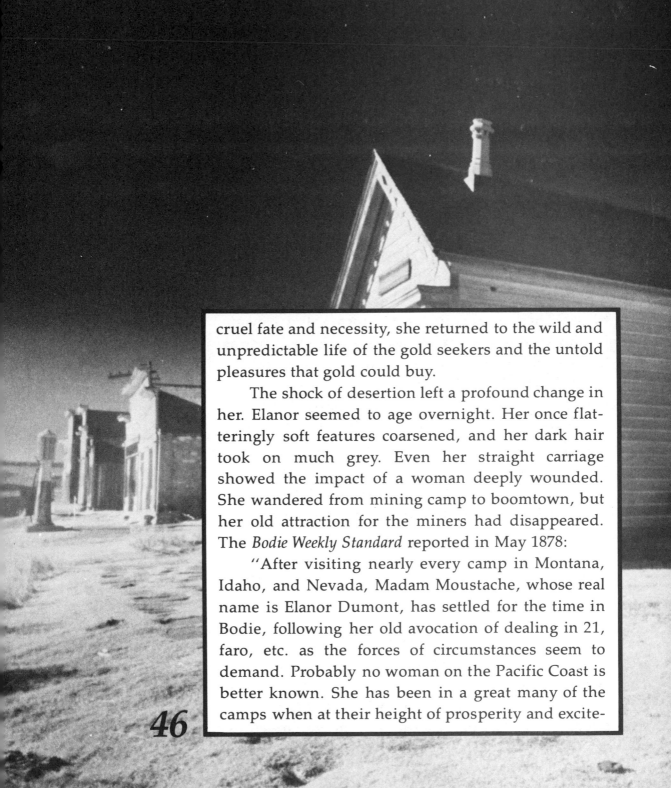

cruel fate and necessity, she returned to the wild and unpredictable life of the gold seekers and the untold pleasures that gold could buy.

The shock of desertion left a profound change in her. Elanor seemed to age overnight. Her once flatteringly soft features coarsened, and her dark hair took on much grey. Even her straight carriage showed the impact of a woman deeply wounded. She wandered from mining camp to boomtown, but her old attraction for the miners had disappeared. The *Bodie Weekly Standard* reported in May 1878:

"After visiting nearly every camp in Montana, Idaho, and Nevada, Madam Moustache, whose real name is Elanor Dumont, has settled for the time in Bodie, following her old avocation of dealing in 21, faro, etc. as the forces of circumstances seem to demand. Probably no woman on the Pacific Coast is better known. She has been in a great many of the camps when at their height of prosperity and excite-

ment and remained until there hardly was a dog there to wail out the dismal story of their desertion. She appears as young as ever, and those who knew her ever so many years ago would instantly recognize her now."

While being sympathetic, the article, according to other reports, exaggerated her appearance. The dark hair that grew on her upper lip was now striking, in contrast to her pallid and aging skin, and the beauty that once would have rebuffed such trivial criticism was now gone. She was known henceforth as Madam Moustache, and not in too kindly a way.

With her gambling skill gone, she was now forced into other pursuits. Using young women to entice men into her games, she used her personal charms to satisfy their other desires. She lived in a wooden house in the most glamorous and notorious of Bodie's "red-light" districts, where the two main streets were, ironically, Maiden Lane and Virgin Alley. She frequented the saloons and dressed in the gaudy styles of the times. Yet skill and fortune failed her.

Slowly Elanor Dumont was cast into the fate of all lost women. She borrowed money for food and lived in abject poverty, caring little for her appearance, her surroundings, or her friends.

A year after her arrival in Bodie, Elanor had "hit bottom." In the small wooden shack perched on the barren slopes outside Bodie she came face to face with the reality of her existence. Alone, unattractive, forgotten, she thought solemnly about the future. What did it hold in store for her? Certainly the town of Bodie was boiling over with gold fever and money for all. There were still plenty of men willing to gamble and drink away their earnings. But she had no luck with them. And was this what she had really wanted from life?

"It didn't seem to matter when I was a girl," she thought, sitting on the edge of a ratty chair left behind by some other gold seeker. "Whoever thought about the next day? It was 'Live today, grab all you can get! Spend it on fine clothes, high-heeled shoes with silver buckles, soft-colored plumage, bottles of cologne, and nice jewelry."

She shook her head sadly. "Why didn't I save any of it? But I did," she nodded, "only to give it over to that no-good man I married."

Where were the quick fingers and the alert mind that had fleeced the miners at cards? Where were the winning smiles that had made them turn over their losses so easily?

"It's all gone. All gone," Elanor thought, soft, warm tears welling in her once sparkling brown eyes. "I've lost my control, my talents, and now my looks."

Hope faded into the icy night wind that howled across the bleak slopes, pushing a tumbleweed along an aimless path. Elanor shivered, filled with the unfamiliar fears of loneliness and failure.

The following day, September 8, 1879, her notoriety made its final newspaper headlines: "The cold remains of Elanor Dumont, also known as Madam Moustache, were found this morning. A bottle of poison was nearby."

LOLA MONTEZ

FROM COURTESAN TO GRASS VALLEY SOCIALITE

"Lola Montez, the artiste, the politician, [member of] the noblesse, and the 'fair shoulder striker' is among us, and her name has attracted to the American Theatre the most brilliant and overflowing audiences ever witnessed in this city, [audiences] who have given her talents a most unequivocal endorsement by the cordial manner in which she has been received. We can't say that we admire Lola's acting, but we do think her dancing is 'heavenly.'" *The Golden Era*, May 29, 1853.

Maria Dolores Eliza Rosanna Gilbert stood in front of a floor-standing gold mirror, studying her fine ivory features, dazzling blue eyes and well-shaped body. At 35, her thick black hair still sparkled like tiny jet beads, and her smile could be subtle or bewitching by choice. She turned one white shoulder and critically surveyed a voluptuous bosom and pinched waist. Without hesitation, she decided she was still an alluring young woman.

Yet at the opening of her San Francisco engagement the night before, all had not gone well. The critics (Damn those people who so freely criticized her acting!) had not taken kindly to her characterization of Lady Teazle in "The School for Scandal." One had dared to say, "She lacked the dignity, subtle wit, voice, and response needed." Another had written, "Everyone knew she was by no means a nice and proper person, yet we were anxious to see her dancing . . . she was wanting in grace and artistic fashion."

Not a woman to be taken lightly or criticized, Dolores Eliza, now simply Lola Montez, Countess of Landsfeld, Spanish dancer and extraordinary beauty, would captivate the audience one way or another. Tonight she would make those same critics choke on their caustic words.

Following the first act of the play "Yelva," Lola caught the audience by surprise. Pirouetting into view, her long, slender legs clad in flesh-colored tights, her glossy hair wreathed in flowers and cascading to her shoulders, with layers of tinted chiffon skirting her waist, and wearing a skintight bodice, Lola Montez writhed into her famous sensuous "Spider Dance."

Some of the audience was repulsed, others thought it erotic, and more found it exciting and entertaining. The chiffon created an illusion of a spider's web, entrapping the dancer as she spun around, constricting her steps and tormenting her emotions. With the dance becoming more frantic, Lola shed stage-prop spiders made of cork and stamped them underfoot. Then the music suddenly changed to a jig and Lola spread her hands and feet out like a huge spider, leaping from one side of the stage to the other. The display ended with total abandonment, as she stamped on the last fallen spider.

The audience, now on its feet, went mad with rapture, shouting "Bravo!" and clamoring for more. Lola Montez had learned that a sagging performance could be enlivened with the "Spider Dance," and San Francisco audiences were witness to this triumph.

As the critics wrote afterwards: "She appeared

last evening before one of the largest audiences ever assembled within the walls of the American Theatre. The principal attraction of the evening was the celebrated 'Spider Dance,' in the execution of which it has been proclaimed Lola has no equal. An unusual degree of excitement prevailed to witness this performance. M'lle Lola appeared in the picturesque costume of 'La Tarantella,' the "Spider Dance" was seen, admired, and encored, and the triumphant danseuse retired amidst showers of bouquets and thunderous applause, after returning thanks in appropriate terms for her kind reception. Her style of dancing is fresh, novel, eccentric, and beautiful, and we cannot doubt she will become an immense favorite as a danseuse." *San Francisco Herald*, May 29, 1853.

Not the Spanish blue blood she claimed to be

☆ ☆ ☆ ☆ ☆ ☆

Born in Limerick, Ireland in 1818, Lola Montez was anything but the Spanish blue blood she claimed to be in later years. She was the daughter of 13-year-old Elizabeth Gilbert (of Spanish or Creole descent) and her young soldier husband, Edward Gilbert. Elizabeth was a beautiful raven-haired woman.

The family lived in India while Lola was a child, and she became the pet of the East India regiments. From her earliest years she spoke freely in Hindustani and Bengali as well as in English. She learned the protocol of army life and became accustomed to the differences in race and color. She found it easy to imitate the slow ritualistic dances of the Indians and enjoyed their food and culture. But when her father died suddenly of cholera, Lola was confronted with the uncertainty of a new father and its certain complications. Though her stepfather, Captain John Craigie, appeared to take her side, she turned against her mother and was sent to Scotland to be reared by relatives.

The child found Scotland much different from India and the worldly excitement of army life. She was placed with relatives in a tightly drawn religious and scholarly household. Lola missed the tropics and her army friends, and found adapting to Scottish schools difficult. While her mastery of languages was excellent, she was not a student to spend hours practicing other lessons. Inevitably she rebelled, and was removed to the family of Sir Jasper Nichols of London.

When she was either 14 or 19 (Lola later changed her birth date), her mother returned with plans to have the child marry Sir Abraham Lumly, judge of the Supreme Court of India, then 60 years old. Lola screamed and cried and a lasting break came between mother and daughter. In a fit of despair, she wed Lieutenant Thomas James of the 21st Regiment of Native Infantry and traveled with him to India, where he was stationed.

During a lecture some years later, Lola said of this, "Runaway matches, like runaway horses, are almost sure to end up in a smash-up. My advice to all young girls who contemplate taking such a step is that they had better hang or drown themselves just one hour before they start."

These must be seen as turbulent years for the young and beautiful woman, who enjoyed the company of other men as did her husband enjoy other women. It was this that caused the couple to ultimately seek divorce. Though it was granted, remarriage was forbidden while either one lived.

On her return voyage from India, Lola took up with a handsome army captain, and their affair soon became the talk of the shipboard travelers. She was shunned by former friends of her parents. However, others encouraged her to take up dancing. They had noticed how easily and gracefully she adapted to the dance floor.

In 1843, when she made her stage debut, she had powerful backing, especially from Lord Malmesbury of the Foreign Office and from Lord Broughan, friend and guardian.

Lola knew how to capture the newspaper reviewers as well, and she soon became a friend of Charles G. Rosenberg, music critic for a London newspaper. Having now split up with Captain Lennox, her shipboard romance, she took rooms across from the music critic. He noted in his column that "she was airy and graceful, with faultless feet and ankles." Yet he also noted she was "good" but "not good enough."

Lola attempted to polish her dancing skills, spending a short time in Spain learning various native dances and customs. It was after this visit that she assumed the name Lola Montez, embellishing her natural origin. She described herself as the daughter of a certain famous Spanish matador. When he denied this, she said she was born in Seville in 1823, the daughter of a Spanish soldier in the service of Don Carlos.

Following her unsuccessful try at the London theatre, Lola went abroad, first to Berlin, then to Munich and Warsaw, and always in the company of a noble gentleman of means and prominent position.

Impulsive and ambitious, Lola was brilliant in all respects, except where her dancing was concerned. She hated the self-denial required of a ballet dancer, and realized that her work lacked polish. It was as if she were rushing through life, seeking success and power, but never having the time to spend polishing the skills needed to get them.

Gaining easy access to the royal courts of Europe, due in part to her dazzling beauty and the manners learned from a childhood spent in Indian army circles, Lola moved from one royal audience to another. Her affairs with minor princes became well publicized, and her dancing ensured quick access to the throne no matter where she went.

It was during a dancing engagement at the Royal Theatre in Dresden that Lola became acquainted with composer Franz Liszt. He was at the height of his fame and was tiring of his current mistress, Comtesse d'Agoult.

Franz Liszt

The liaison between Lola and Liszt became a topic of gossip across two continents. Newspaper columnists wrote vivid accounts of their adventures, often with an underlying espionage theme. Was Lola Montez spying for one of the radical groups sweeping through Europe? Richard Wagner was known to have befriended Liszt, and Paris cafes overflowed with the new breed. While her spying was often implied, in her later memoirs Lola never admitted to

such activities. Liszt adored her and she him, it was said. But he also found the tempestuous dancer maddening and distracting.

Lola's intense passion for publicity did not help the romance. At the Beethoven Festival in Bonn in the summer of 1845, their tempers were aroused over a speech Liszt had given. A shouting match commenced and was climaxed by Lola's jumping to a table, capturing center stage. Liszt had her locked in her room until he left. The romance cooled afterward, and Liszt was known to have told friends "too great were her demands and her indifference to my work."

From Germany, Lola appears to have gone to Turkey, where another socially prominent individual, Sir Stratford Canning, gave her backing and introductions to royal circles. She performed there, but returned to Paris soon thereafter.

Lola had a keen sense for public relations even in those days, and she was always quick to befriend a journalist or visiting newspaper publisher. In Paris, she became a friend of Alexander Dumas, whose serialization of the "Count of Monte Cristo" was one of the most popular stories of the day. Dumas found Lola exciting and intelligent, full of wit and worldly knowledge. Through him, she was introduced to Alexander Henri Dujarier, editor of *La Presse*. Dujarier immediately endorsed her talents despite her stage failures, and another romantic affair commenced.

☜ *Portrait of Lola Montez during her European days*

What made Lola Montez an accomplished courtesan and world personality? Perhaps it was her status in the community in which she traveled. It may even have been her violent temper and outspoken methods. But it was certainly not her dancing—reviews were seldom favorable. Yet it was always noted that she was a dramatic beauty and a fine conversationalist. The time she spent mixing with the literary and artistic personalities of foreign countries also did much to further her career.

While living in Paris, Lola attended all the fashionable theatres and cafes and the opera, mixing with the genuises of the time. Balzac, Victor Hugo, and Alfred de Musset were but a few. Revolutionists abounded and spoke out freely against the royal cliques. Lola spent much time in endless political discussions with these men of radical views, and was a dominant figure at the smart, private salons of Paris. With an alert interest in politics, Lola found she could hold her own with many a man, and her judgments and political perceptions were often well received.

Here she also met George Sand, famous novelist and nonconformist, and followed her lead, taking up cigar smoking and showing strong feminist inclinations. In Paris, the intellectual qualities of women went further than anywhere else, and Lola devoured it all. From these famous personalities she acquired acute intelligence; nevertheless, her emotions were, at times, still uncontrolled.

During this period of her life, she became the

She could hold her own with many a man

★ ★ ★ ★ ★ ★ ★

mistress of Dujarier. But before she could tire of him, he was killed in a duel with a journalist rival. A celebrated trial followed, and Lola once again was the star. Though stunned by Dujarier's death, Lola inherited considerable shares in the Palais Royal Theatre, which enabled her to go to Germany.

At Baden there was a fleeting episode with the Prince of Reuss, but he was unimportant and his dominions too small to hold her. She then made her way to Munich, where she had heard of the amiable but lunatic King Ludwig I of Bavaria. The city was bustling with art and color, largely due to the efforts of the 60-year-old monarch. Women were devout, men were faithful, and the Catholic Church and the Wittelsbach were impregnable institutions.

It is amazing how quickly Lola aroused the antagonism of the city. The king had known her for only two weeks when she danced for the second and last time, and already it was necessary to fill the orchestra pit with policemen to protect her. But the capricious woman with dark beauty and seductive manners had bewitched the old king. He sought her company all the time and wrote poems about their relationship. Soon he was consulting her on matters of state, which alarmed the clerical party.

The Jesuits, shocked by the liaison, demanded that King Ludwig break off the romance. Acting on Lola's advice, Ludwig dismissed his chief minister of control. Other government heads soon fell. Within a year Lola was, in effect, ruling the kingdom as well as the king. He had built her a beautiful home and

had her portrait hung in the Schönheits gallery. He also tried raising her to peerage with the title of Countess of Landsfeld.

But in order to ennoble Lola, a letter of naturalization had to be countersigned by a minister, who refused. The entire cabinet offered the king a choice: their resignations or dismissal of his favorite. King Ludwig dismissed the cabinet, and the Countess of Landsfeld had her hour of triumph.

It should be said that the political struggles taking place all across Europe at this time inflamed the growing feud in Bavaria. The antagonism of the clerical party toward Lola was more than a desire to oust her; it was the old order fighting the rise of young radicals. She was declared a sorceress and called a spy. Tempers at the university became violent, so Ludwig closed the prestigious school, ordering the students home. Munich was shocked and the people petitioned the king to reconsider. Awaiting an answer, the city was now in open insurrection. Mobs demanded that Lola be banished. Up to this point, King Ludwig had stood firmly by her side, Now, however, with his city at war, he surrendered to the people, signing an order that the countess leave the city within an hour.

Lola could not believe Ludwig had deserted her. But as the mob began smashing her windows, threatening her and cursing her very life, she left town. The king never saw her again, although he sent her a royal allowance.

The rioting continued and the king grew bitter

toward the people he had done so much for; the Bavarians wanted more concessions. Three weeks later, Ludwig abdicated his throne.

Meanwhile, the countess traveled across the continent and was soon married to George Trafford Heald, a young corporal in the second regiment of the Life Guards. She was promptly arrested on a charge of bigamy and escaped by forfeiting her bail. Heald, though young, was wealthy. But Lola soon tired of him. Seeking excitement and love and still receiving a small allowance from Ludwig, Lola wrote her memoirs and took up residence in Paris. The manuscript was to be published by Le Pays, but new management dropped the idea.

Disappointed over her debut as an author, Lola was suddenly stricken with influenza. The epidemic raged through the countryside that spring of 1851, killing many and leaving Lola bald and depressingly thin and weak.

Badgered by creditors, physically not well, and perhaps feeling like a failure at 33, Lola did some serious thinking about her future. She arranged a European tour and was determined to be professional and tolerant. Perfecting her talents, learning six new dances, Lola was ready. But her hopes were dimmed when she learned that young Heald had drowned. Lola wept sadly, realizing her path had once more been crossed by violence.

By November of 1851 she had returned from a successful theatrical tour unmarred by ugly reviews and sudden bouts of temper. Exhausted, she settled **63** back in Paris, talking to American friends about the land of independence and the chances of her success in a new country.

Promotor Phineas T. Barnum, building up a touring company of stars, wanted to sign Lola on as a client. But when she heard he had referred to her as "notorious" she declined. Instead, she enlisted the aid of Edward Willis to manage her engagements.

Famed as political reformer

★ ★ ★ ★ ★ ★ ★

Coming to America, Lola had planned to change her image and be accepted as a political reformer who had played a part in the revolutions sweeping Europe. Yet her fame as a dazzling beauty, committed to passion and uproar, followed her across the Atlantic. She could work wonders with the men who interviewed her, but her name and royal escapades were too well-known not to reach the public's ears.

Her first performance in New York City was met with bad reviews. She had trouble keeping time with the music, and her dancing was not as perfect as that of others who had delighted the eastern stage. Her tendency to get into print did not help. Lola got into fights with reviewers and management and was soon involved in a fresh new scandal: leaving her lodgings without settling the bill. Moving again and redoing her quarters lavishly, Lola's new life was reminiscent of the Paris days. Yet luck was against her, and she was soon evicted from her home. Still full of high hopes and with an indomitable spirit, Lola set off on a tour of Philadelphia, Boston, Washington, New Orleans, and the West Coast. She was met with the same critical assaults, accused of "making a mockery

PANAMA RAILROAD.

65

of the art which was cultivated by the famous, and her attempts at acting [are] ludicrous."

In New Orleans she was well received, and encountered only minor trouble with critics and police. Leaving for California, Lola must have hoped the bold new West would hold the key to her happiness.

Arriving in San Francisco, it did not take the newspapers or her critics long to begin their vicious attacks. And Lola, true to form, was soon battling audiences as well as the press. She was quickly recognized wherever she went, and was even caricatured. Headlines proclaimed her to be in many entanglements and gossip was rampant.

While crossing the isthmus of Panama, she had gained two new suitors, both newspapermen: Samuel Brannan of the *California Star* and Patrick Purdy Hull, later part-owner of *The Whig*. Both were captivated by her dazzling beauty and worldly intellect. But it was Hull she married, after a short engagement in San Francisco. Immediately after their wedding, the couple set off on a tour of Sacramento and the nearby gold mining camps.

In her lectures, years later, Lola was intensely critical of American men. She said, "They were not at home except to sleep, and they were so absorbed in the rise and fall of stocks that they had no affection to give their families. . . Thus love became a business like everything else. . . Men manipulated pretty women as they did stocks. . . ."

Needless to say, Lola and Hull were soon fighting in public, and her stage appearances suffered

Lola's house in Grass Valley, Nevada

badly. It was at this time that she dropped the role of actress and confined herself to the "Spider Dance," "Sailor's Hornpipe," and a Swiss dance complete with yodeling. Violinist Miska Hauser, traveling with her as accompanist, stopped many a cabbage-throwing crowd with patriotic salutes. Lola would come to his aid, silencing the audiences with defiant words and seductive smiles.

Marital problems reached their peak when an engraved gold comb from King Ludwig arrived while the couple was in Marysville. Hull accused his wife of all types of deceit, and she retaliated by tossing his clothes out the hotel window.

The beautiful and picturesque mining town of Grass Valley was the last stop on her tour. It was another Bavaria, with snow-covered mountain peaks and thick pine groves. It was also the settling spot of the famous courtesan.

67

Lola built a home and decorated it lavishly, entertaining guests with no heed to expenses. Her European friends soon swarmed about her, as did the robust miners. She raised and cared for animals, including a bear cub, and tended to a garden. As usual, there were people opposed to her ways, but Lola made the best of it. It was here she was welcomed into the bohemian circle that also included the mother of Lotta Crabtree. Lola was fascinated with the child and taught her horseback riding and dancing. Lotta in turn adored the countess, and would visit her house regularly to eat Bavarian pastries and dress up in her fine European costumes. But when Lola planned a tour of Australia, Lotta's mother would not allow the child to go with her. Lola was openly disappointed, but set out on the trip with the same high spirits she constantly maintained.

Accompanying her was a young man named Augustus Noel Follin, married and the father of three children but still enraptured with the Countess. He signed on as her agent. But in writing to his relatives, he let it be known that he found the former mistress of the King of Bavaria exciting.

When she returned to the United States, Lola knew her stage days were coming to an end. After a short engagement doing a sister act with Follin's young daughter, Miriam, Lola retired. She continued to hold court for many politicians and celebrities of the day.

★ ★ ★ ★ ★ ★ ★

Lola champions

women's rights

Early in 1858 Lola Montez became a champion for women's rights, taking to the lecture circuit. She traveled extensively, giving beauty advice, making critical comments about men in general, and constantly denying that she was immoral. Women found her beauty tips interesting and also enjoyed the book she published on the matter, *The Arts of Beauty, or Secrets of a Lady's Toilet with Hints to Gentlemen on The Art of Fascinating*.

At 40, ravaged by her turbulent life and full of disillusionment, Lola took up the Bible, hoping to do penance for all her past sins. She was converted to Methodism and roamed through the New York parks, reading and quoting the scriptures. Her health was failing, and her money was gone. During her final days, she was taken in and cared for by Mrs. Margaret Buckanan, a childhood friend from Scotland. Dr. Francis Hawks cared for her religious needs, and she told him of her intense hatred of her mother and the miserable life she had as a child. Dr. Hawks wrote up her story, and *The Story of a Penitent* was published by the Protestant Episcopal Society.

Lola died quietly on January 17, 1861. She was buried in the Greenwood Cemetery in New York. Her estate had only enough money to pay her funeral expenses and to make a small donation to the Madadlen Asylum for Women.

Perhaps her own words, presented in one of her lectures, best described her tumultuous life. "The great misfortune was that there was too much of me to be held within the prescribed and safe limits allotted to woman; but there was not enough to enable me to stand securely beyond the shelter of conventional rules."

5

ROSITA AND DORINA

FIVE SENSELESS MURDERS

nlike the other women in this historical collection, Rosita Felix de Murietta and Dorina Brennan were neither single nor celebrated. They were the wives of ambitious men who came to California seeking their fortunes in the gold fields. Rosita was childless and Spanish, while Dorina was Irish and the mother of three small children. Both endured the many hardships of the mining camps, and in the end died violently and without purpose. Their short lives were but a few of the tragedies of the Gold Rush.

Born into a well-to-do Castilian family which had settled a few years before in Hermosillo, Mexico Rosita had been reared to a life of ease. Her days were spent at the grey Felix rancho, situated near the sienna foothills of Sonora. Here was the little church where she daily said her prayers, and the outdoor ovens where servants prepared tortillas and special delights. Like other young women, she enjoyed taking part in the holiday fiestas, riding horseback, and embroidering colorful designs on her garments. At 17 she fell in love for the first and only time with a handsome young man named Joaquin Murietta.

Of Spanish Basque heritage, the Murietta family had come from the Pyrenees, receiving a grant of land in Hermosillo. Late in the eighteenth century they were driven from this land by Yaquis and Apaches, who had swept in from the north. But Joaquin was eager to restore his family's wealth and position. He also wanted Rosita by his side.

"Rosita," he said, his dark eyes attentive to her every move, "won't you please marry me?"

The young girl's creamy cheeks flushed, her long black eyelashes dipped softly. "But what would Father say?" And then before Joaquin could reply, she broke into a whimsical imitation of her parent. "A nobody," she said, stamping her foot. "That's what he is. Did I bring you up to marry a vaquero? I want something much more for my beautiful daughter. A husband who can give you a big hacienda and lots of servants to care for you."

Young Joaquin shook his head fiercely. "No, Rosita. He wants you to be happy. And with me you will be the happiest girl in this whole world."

"Perhaps I shouldn't see you anymore, Joaquin," she said teasingly. "Perhaps you should go away."

"But I *am* going away, Rosita. I'm going to California to seek gold. My brother, Jesus, writes that the rivers of California are just begging for me to scoop the dazzling nuggets from their rocky beds. That's why you must marry me and come with me to California."

Rosita wrinkled her wide brow, frightened at the thought of leaving her lovely home and traveling so far by ship to a strange land inhabited by foreigners. The war with the United States had just ended, and Mexico had been forced to give up California, Utah, Nevada, parts of Colorado, Wyoming, and New Mexico. Rosita had seen those white-faced soldiers who rode with fury, ate pickles and pie, and drank English tea. They had scared her then, and the dark moments still clung in her mind. Yet her love for the passionate Joaquin was more than she could bear, and the thought of losing him quickly changed her mind. She would go with him, no matter where, with or without her parents' consent.

Señor Felix, however, was wise to the ways of his daughter, and her love for the adventurous cowboy soon won out. He consented to their union, and shortly thereafter they were married in the little white church of Hermosillo. Rosita wore a simple cloth dress with a gold embroidered shawl, and an exquisite lace mantilla fell over her shoulders. Heaven shone in her lustrous eyes as she thought of Joaquin, kneeling beside her.

That afternoon they rode down the hills from the village toward the Gulf of California. The horse galloped magnificently; Joaquin's red sash blew in the light wind, his straw hat pushed to the back of his black, curly hair. Behind him sat Rosita, her warm arms clinging about her lover's waist.

They sailed the gulf, rounding Lower (Baja) California, then commenced northward to San Francisco, the entrance to the gold country. Holding hands, they smiled attentively at each other, Rosita unaware that anything else but love mattered. Joaquin, also captured by romance, dreamed of a long life with Rosita, but he also thought about the new land and its easy riches.

In the bustling and booming bay city, they soon found other friends from Sonora. Mexican women in traditional black and men in bright shirts and sandaled feet all laughed and talked about their new homes and the gold to the east. There were foreigners of all sorts, Chinese, Italians, Irish, and French, and the native Indians. Within the city whiskey was plentiful, and gambling was a quick way to lose a day's wages from the diggings.

Some of the younger women had turned to prostitution to get wealthy, or in some cases, to survive. They dressed in gaudy satins and taffetas and wore dark stockings and high-heeled shoes with brilliant studs. They took up smoking and gambling, forgetting the morals of family and church. But Rosita was not one of them. To the end, she kept her sacred marriage vows and was true to Joaquin. She loved no other.

By crowded steamer, they traveled up the Sacramento River, carrying a pick and shovel like the hundreds of other adventurers that hurried to the creeks and mountains of the Mother Lode. Leaving the boat, they purchased a mule and food and headed northward to the town of Sonora. Perhaps, because this new camp had been named for their home, the Muriettas thought it lucky. Joaquin would strike it rich, and in Rosita's mind, the couple would return to Mexico. But Sonora's claims had all been staked, so they moved on, camping along the crystal creeks and later along the beautiful Stanislaus River.

That year the California legislature passed the Foreign Miners Tax Law, which imposed a levy of $20 every thirty days on all foreign miners. Joaquin paid this from money he had brought with him and from what he won at gambling, a pastime he now enjoyed.

Up the Sacramento River with pick and shovel

✸ ✸ ✸ ✸ ✸ ✸

The young Mexicans proudly staked out fifteen square feet, their share of this new land in the steep mountains of the Sierra Nevada range. They slept under a dome of brilliant stars that dotted the heavens.

According to one newspaper account, Joaquin was one day approached by Irish miners and ordered off his claim. When he resisted, he was beaten, flogged, and robbed by them, losing $4,000. Later he was run off again by Americans, and this time one drunken miner smashed a bottle in his face. It is recorded that his wounds were treated by a Colonel Acklen.

After these ruthless encounters with Yankee miners, Rosita and Joaquin grew disillusioned with the gold country. But rather than go back to Mexico, Joaquin decided to try his luck with cards.

Crossing the Calaveras River, they journeyed northward to the town of Murphy's Camp. However, Joaquin's dream of riches was dealt another severe blow. Setting up his tent in the tree-shaded camp, Joaquin operated a "monte" game. Rosita tended to their cooking, laughing and singing with the other Mexicans. But once again the couple was taunted by American miners, who were jealous of any success Mexicans might have. A group of tough and drunken fellows tore down the tent, sending Joaquin and Rosita fleeing to the river's edge. Alone again, they were ready to call it quits.

The afternoon was warm. A dry wind was rustling through the canyons, wafting the scents of sage and oak. Joaquin waded into the splashing waters

75

and scooped up a panful of black sand. He stirred it with his finger. Suddenly he cried out.

"Rosita, come quickly. Look, I have found gold! We are rich! Now we can return to Hermosillo, and your father will be proud of me."

Rosita waded into the clear water, holding her skirts above her knees.

"I'm so happy, Joaquin. Yes, now we can go home."

The couple laughed and sang loudly, rejoicing at their discovery. On the shaded bank of the stream, eight Americans heard the familiar cheer. They stormed through the waters and splashed up the muddy banks to Rosita and Joaquin's camp.

"So you struck gold," one said angrily. He was wearing a red shirt and slouching hat. "Let's see it."

Cautiously Joaquin revealed his find, uncertain what the miner's reactions might be.

The grubby crew stared at the tiny nuggets of bright yellow, mumbling to each other. Finally one ordered, "Get off this land, Mexican. It's ours now."

The other men kicked at the makeshift cooking stove where Rosita had been making tortillas, tossing them into the fire. Another one reached out to grab her.

Rosita, frightened of the strangers, stepped back, tripping on a rock.

"Leave her alone," Joaquin shouted. "I have paid my tax for this claim. It is mine."

"Who says so?" a heavy, unshaven man spit. "Foreigners don't own land in California."

"Yes, yes," Joaquin said. "I paid my taxes. It's my claim."

"We'll see who's claim it is," the men shouted, pulling guns and baring fists.

Rosita cried out again.

Joaquin fought until his eyes were clouded with blood and his senses unbalanced, but he was outnumbered. He was aware of being smashed against the rocky terrain, but only for a short moment. For a long time he lay unconscious, reliving in his mind the nightmare of violence and humiliation he and his beloved Rosita had endured. Her father had been right; she should not have married him. But they loved each other, and he was certain he could make a good life for her. Again his head whirled, his vision blurring. But he was strong and would not die.

He awoke, dried blood clotting his eyes and face and clothes. "Rosita," he called out. "Rosita."

Suddenly he heard a crying little whisper. "Joaquin, please let me die. Please."

Rosita lay in a clump of bushes, assaulted, strangled, and near death.

"Oh, no," Joaquin sobbed, seeing his beautiful wife covered with her own blood, her clothes torn from her body. "Please, Rosita. You must live. I love you."

"No, Joaquin," she gasped, breathing faintly. "I must die."

Joaquin held her gently in his arms, staining her soft cheeks with his tears. All night he held her close, the strange sounds of the rustling hills his only com-

77

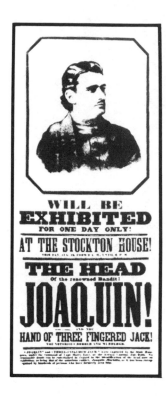

pany. By morning Rosita was dead, a peaceful smile on her face, her white limbs cold.

Joaquin wrapped her in the gold embroidered shawl and buried her body in the rich earth of California. He prayed to the Virgin Mary to always take care of his Rosita.

Tormented by the senseless murder of his wife and by the ugly acts of violence he had experienced, Joaquin Murietta went on to become one of the most notorious bandits of the Gold Rush era. His reign of terror came to an end in July 1853: he was shot in the back by rangers commissioned by the state to seek him out. His head was severed from his body and for many years was displayed across the country. It came to rest in a San Francisco museum, and there, during the great earthquake of 1906, it was destroyed by fire.

In 1949, an old grave marker was found in a pile of rubbish near Murphy's Creek. Carved into the wood was the still-legible epitaph: "Mrs. Joaquin Murietta. Died in 1852. Rest in Peace."

Dorina Brennan, a pretty Irish lass with striking red hair and twinkling brown eyes, was 27 years old when she and her husband Michael came to California. Leaving a comfortable brick home in New York City and a good position on the editorial staff of the *Daily Press*, Michael, like thousands of other men, dreamed only of gold. He also had plans to one day bring his mother and sister to America from their home in Ireland.

Like her husband, Dorina had been born in Ireland and brought up with a deep regard for family and God. She often missed the rolling green hills and the bright wild flowers that splashed across the eastern countryside every spring. But it was her duty to stay by her husband's side, even after he decided to move her and their two children from New York to Grass Valley, California.

"Well," she said, smiling at her small children, "Daddy is at least going to have a job when we get there."

He would indeed have work. Michael had been employed by the Mount Hope Mining Company to superintend the company's operations on the newly constructed Massachusetts Hill Mine.

The long journey from New York to California had not been easy for Dorina, who was already expecting her third child. Even Elle, 5, and Rob, 3, often tired of the trips. But despite the hardships of overland travel, the Brennans arrived safely in Grass Valley in 1856.

That winter, snow capped the Sierra Nevadas, and a strong, piercing wind blew through the folds of the high mountains, filling the log cabins and tents with a bone-tingling cold. Despite the poor weather, the town was rapidly growing. The city already measured one square mile, the center being the junction of Broad and Pine Streets. A new hotel, the Monumental, had been opened in December and the local government was proceeding better than expected. In the fall election, over 2,000 people turned out, a number exceeded only in San Francisco and Sacramento. And six miles above the city, a new dam was being planned to provide a reservoir.

Michael spent much of his time at the mine, trying to make it more productive. Dorina, meanwhile, made friends with her new neighbors, setting up housekeeping in a small wooden cabin close to town. The few things she had brought with her were treasured and used daily.

The first summer was exciting and rewarding for the entire family. Little Dorina was born, healthy and well, and the mine appeared to be doing fine. Despite the difficulties of pioneer life, Dorina collected wild berries to flavor her meals and gathered mustard greens, sprigs of dock, and other native plants known for their medicinal as well as nutritional values. She planted a garden, and fruits and vegetables were dried for the next winter's use.

But as 1857 neared, Michael's personal invest-

There were few moments of rest for miners ☞

ments began to dry up, and the mine was not producing as much ore as had been as expected.

After dinner one evening, with the three children tucked in bed, Michael spoke to Dorina of his
failures. A tiny fire glowed in the open fireplace. The
evening meal had been sparse, due to his suggestion
that they had better save up for the bleak months
ahead.

The haggard man looked at his pretty wife, her
once bright eyes dulled from work and caring for
three small children, her once supple body tired and
frail.

"Perhaps we should go back east," he said, his
face sullen.

Dorina was pensive, noticing the slight twitch
developing in her husband's hands.

"I just don't think I'm going to make a go of the
mining business. Perhaps someone with more fore-
sight and skill could do better at it."

"You mustn't blame yourself, Michael," Dorina
said smiling. "It's not your fault the mine is not living up to expectations. It takes time. Just wait and
see. By spring everything will be going well."

"I'm not so sure, Dorina. It seems we go from
bad to worse. We don't even have enough food. And
here I had promised you riches beyond belief."

"Now, Michael, you are my husband and the
father of our three wonderful children. That's enough
for me."

82 Michael shook his head. He was a proud man
who did not take defeat easily. "No," he said, "It's

me. I'm not doing the right thing. Something is wrong, but I just don't know how to right it."

At nearly 30, Michael Brennan appeared anguished. His light hair was thinning, and his deeply set eyes and narrow mouth were pale and expressionless.

"In the spring, Michael," Dorina said, trying to reassure him, "everything will be fine. It's just that the weather hasn't been good, and the cold and rain make everyone feel poorly. When spring comes and the flowers bloom, you'll feel better. Now come, let's go to bed where it's warm."

"I wish I had your optimism, Dorina," he said, looking about the barren room of the cabin. "I wanted to buy you so many nice things, and bring Momma and my sister to America. But it doesn't look like that will ever happen."

"Of course it will, Michael. You just have to have hope in this land. Why, every day someone is digging up a gold nugget as big as your fist. Just you wait, the mine will prove out alright."

But Michael had already decided he was a failure, and all of Dorina's encouragement could not bring him out of his agony.

Dorina said nothing more, for she was sure in her own heart that the new year would be better. She never missed New York City and its freezing winters, or the affluent life they had there. Grass Valley was beautiful, and often, with its mountains capped in snow, she was reminded of a fairy-tale book she had seen once in the East. She mustn't lose sight of

83

her dream that someday all would be well with the Brennan family.

Despite her optimism, the year dawned badly. Andre Chevanne, who held the mine's mortgage, was about to foreclose, and Michael blamed himself even more for the mine's failure. Dorina tried to coax her husband into a better frame of mind, but it was useless. He was determined to blame himself.

During the first week in February, Michael sought out an attorney, A. B. Dibble. It was his intention to have a will drawn up.

"You're really much too young a man to be worried about dying," Dibble said on the first visit.

"It's always well to protect one's family," Michael returned. "One never can predict tomorrow."

"Well, of course," Dibble added. "And will-drawing is part of my business. But nevertheless you are a young man in the best of health and with a job."

"A bad lot at that," Michael said.

"But most of the men here have no permanent position. They live from day to day on what they might bring from the ground. And then many of them take it all and throw it away on the gambling tables or corn whiskey. I sometimes wonder what this country is coming to."

"I have made my plans," Michael said, ignoring the attorney's mumbling. "I want my affairs in order for whatever happens."

"Whatever you say, Mr. Brennan. After all, you're paying the bill."

Dibble promised to have all the documents drawn up soon so that Michael could return to sign them. Michael said nothing and left the office solemnly.

Later Dibble told friends that he thought Michael Brennan was "slightly insane." He didn't know one other man in Grass Valley who was worried about dying. Rather, they were worried about not getting their claim staked in time.

The will was drawn and Michael signed it. It was soon afterwards that he received a letter from Andre Chevanne saying that because of the poor profits, he would soon be foreclosing on the company.

Brennan's melancholy turned from bad to worse. He blamed himself for everything that had gone wrong.

"Now, now, Michael," Dorina again tried to make him smile. "Things will be better. Perhaps we should go down to Sacramento. Maybe you could find a job there where the pressure wouldn't be so bad."

Michael sat in the corner chair, his head lowered, eyes colorless, his face without expression. He had failed. He knew for a fact that other men would have made the mine a success. All through the mountains miners were discovering gold, some nuggets being as large as silver dollars, but he couldn't find anything.

Every day they toiled in the mine. Michael was sure that blasting sections would yield a million or so in revenue. But every day ended in failure.

Michael was beside himself. What had gone

wrong? Where had his dream failed him? Was he so stupid that he couldn't do anything successfully? He had battled for two years, but his operations had proved disastrous. Yet he knew he'd once had a fine mind—and he'd used it well at the newspaper to land this position with the mining company. No, he thought, why think of this company? He had failed them, losing thousands of dollars in the attempt to locate gold ore. Each day was growing worse. He could not shake his feelings of guilt and despair.

On Saturday, February 21, 1858, Michael Brennan took his last few coins and stopped at the local market for wine. It had been a long day at the mine, and still no gold. No gold! That was all he could think about. All over town miners were panning for gold in the streams and digging in makeshift holes in the hills, yet he, in his big mine, with much help and money from the East, could not strike a single golden vein.

He took the wine in his arms.

"Have a good Sunday," the shopkeeper called. "And say hello to the Mrs. That's one fine Irish lass you have there, and those three little children are as dear as the Blarney stone itself."

Michael did not acknowledge the shopkeeper. Instead, he walked silently out of the store, his mind a million miles away.

That night Dorina fixed a fine meal of beans and salt pork. The children played noisily in the small room, laughing and chattering as youngsters do. Michael watched them, his eyes and mouth twisted in sadness. How young, how innocent they were.

Who would take care of them if they suddenly had no mother or father, he thought.

Then he knew exactly what must be done. In a delirious state, he poured wine for the family, turning his back to the commotion of game playing. Dorina, who was cleaning up the dishes, did not notice that he dropped prussic acid into the wine.

"Now," he said, in only what could be called an insane calmness. "We must toast our future, Mommy's and Daddy's. And how we will all be together no matter what happens."

Dorina smiled with her familiar Irish twinkle. "I'm glad you think of us as one, Michael. You know we will always be here, wanting to take care of you and love you."

Michael smiled, his lips curling with bitterness. How could he leave his loving family in this remote and violent camp without him? His wife would have to turn to prostitution or drink. And what would happen to the children? They would become orphans, hungry and cold; cast out of society, they might turn to stealing or something far worse. They must be with their father. Only he could take care of them.

"Let's drink to our future," he said, as Dorina gathered the children up for bed. "One last sip for tomorrow and what it will bring."

"Well, if you insist, Michael," Dorina said. "But the children are getting tired, so please hurry. Besides, the fire will be out soon, and the cold will be coming in."

On Sunday morning, a friend stopped by to pass

87

the time of day and found the bodies, cold and rigid in death.

The children were found in different rooms, while Dorina lay on the sofa and her husband on the floor in the parlor. By Michael's side lay a loaded pistol, cocked, though for what purpose one can only surmise.

Michael left a letter fully explaining what had led him to commit this horrible deed. "I do not feel that I have mislead or deceived anyone. But rather Massachusetts Hill is the deceiver. It is cowardly to leave my wife and children behind to face the unknown, so they come with me in death." He added that he wished he could take with him on his long journey his mother and sister still living in Europe, who were dependent upon him for maintenance.

The town was temporarily upset by the unnecessary deaths of the Brennan family. But fate appears to have won another battle with reason. Following the tragedy, Andre Chevanne confirmed the title and took over the mine. The first blast of black powder his new mine foreman used brought down a shower of white fragments, each richly speckled with gold. Mining developed into a major industry in this town, and its operation continued for more than 100 years. In all, over $1 million in rich gold ore poured from the bowels of Massachusetts Hill. Grass Valley became the richest and most famous gold-mining district in California.

Dorina Brennan and Rosita Murietta were but two victims of the many senseless crimes of the mid-1800s. How many more women suffered without reason we shall never know.

Flowers dot the five Brennan graves in Grass Valley, Nevada

EMMA WIXOM

FROM CALIFORNIA TO THE SOPHISTICATED EUROPEAN STAGE

Emma Wixom stood on the balcony of the National Hotel, her arms outstretched, a cold breeze brushing against her pink cheeks, her hazel eyes sparkling. In all her celebrated performances, none of the audiences' reactions had touched her as much as this. Coming home and being jubilantly welcomed by the unsophisticated people of California was heartwarming indeed. The tiny diva, dazzling in a swirl of lace and satin, once more waved to the crowd and applauded the band as it played "Auld Lang Syne."

Emma had returned home. But even this morning, as the narrow-gauge train steamed into the depot, she had never dreamed her welcome would be so tumultuous. Thousands of people cheered as her railroad car pulled in, and the band struck up "Home Sweet Home."

What memories she carried with her, what a world of priceless souvenirs! Her life was brilliant, full of memorable moments. She was a celebrity, the reigning soprano at more than seventy of the leading opera houses of the world. And she was the incontestable mistress of every role she sang, identifying herself with each one she performed. Now this unassuming American lady had come back to Nevada City, and her welcome was unmatched.

Inside her room, always remembered as number 11, were banks of beautiful flowers and notes from well-wishers. Gold and silver satin streamers flut-

Flattering crowds left singer natural and unassuming

✫ ✫ ✫ ✫ ✫ ✫

91

tered from the bouquets. The fragrance was overwhelming. Emma was indeed touched by her welcome, and all the events of her past suddenly filled her mind. It was not so long ago, she recalled, that she gave her first performance. Amateurish as it was, she was headed for success.

Her father, Dr. William Wallace Wixom, was a physician at the Alpha Hydraulic Mine right above the seven hills of Nevada City. Emma was born February 25, 1859, in the small mining camp not far from town called Alpha, one of the best-known gold producers of the northern mines. In the cold winter months, she and her mother, Kate, stayed at a home on East Broad Street. Little is known about her mother, who died when the child was 8 years old, but everyone remembered Emma. By the time she was 3 she had already given a public performance: standing on a chair in church and waving the American flag, she sang the "Star Spangled Banner." Even then, there were those who knew the tiny child had talent.

It was in Alpha that she also learned the finger alphabet of the deaf and dumb in order to talk with Era Adams, a miner who had been deafened by an explosion. Ironically, Adams was Emma's first singing teacher.

After the unexpected death of her mother, it fell to her father, Dr. Wixom, to raise and care for her. Since she was an only child, it was quite natural that her young life was centered largely about her devoted father. In between his daily tasks at the mine, he encouraged her singing and took her to town and church, where the local townspeople found her youthful talent sweet and entertaining. Even as a child, however, Emma was never pretentious, but full of natural grace and charm. In those days she took her warm audiences more as a matter of fact than anything else.

The family moved to the small Nevada town of Austin, and this was their home for some years. Emma was 5 years old when she appeared as the star performer in Austin's International Hall. The local newspaper editor enthusiastically acclaimed her, saying, "Taken all in all, this was by far the best concert we have ever listened to in Austin, and one which will be long remembered."

Dressed in a long gingham dress, Emma sang in doorways along Austin's main street, the sound of her childish treble at times almost drowned by the clatter of silver coins falling about her feet. It was really no wonder that the young state of Nevada claimed the talented songstress. Many people came to believe that she was indeed a native of the state, and she was dubbed Emma Nevada.

As a child she delighted in gathering wild flowers and making wreaths. When the colorful halo was finished, she would place it on her head and then stand boldly in front of a freestanding mirror, singing newly learned arias. Soon she was being called a child prodigy. Even her wreath of flowers was imitated and given a name, the Wixom Halo.

Through all these audacious and flattering out-pourings Emma remained natural and unassuming. Her father was a typical product of his time and

place, living in cheerful poverty. Though buoyed up by the expectation of sudden wealth, he taught his daughter a priceless lesson. Almost from the time she could walk he impressed on her that singing to an audience was as natural a form of amusement as making mud pies, and it was much more profitable. With her inborn ability and her father's confidence, Emma soon gained the self-assurance needed to be a star.

Because of her father's help and dedication, she was able to attend Mills Seminary in Oakland, later known as Mills College. There she studied under the school's German music teacher, Professor Kelleher, and, of course, sang whenever she was asked. This included student activities, faculty gatherings, and the popular Sunday evening musicals.

This period of her celebrated life was well remembered in later years. Her former classmates particularly recalled her unquenchable love of singing. They also recalled, however, that she failed to distinguish herself in classroom activities. And they remembered that while she was not really pretty, she had an attractive, uptilted nose that gave her face a delightfully arch expression, and that she fancied bright colors, wearing them in extraordinary combinations. Moreover, they said, "When she grew too stout for her clothes and burst them out, her style of mending was not the best. . . . She never took kindly to stabbing drygoods with a needle. . . ."

But poor grades and student criticism must not have daunted the young woman. For it was here, at the Sunday night student concerts, that Emma came into her own.

These gatherings brought crowds of people from San Francisco and Oakland. Gathering in the large rooms of the school, they were enraptured with the fine voice of the young singer. One acclaimed it as the "finest to be heard anywhere." Clothes and grades were forgotten.

Emma was nearsighted, and this in itself caused additional admiration. When she sang, "Shall I Wear a White Rose, or Shall I Wear a Red Rose," gazing into the audience with her bright eyes half closed and her pretty mouth wrapped in a most convincing smile, there wasn't a college boy present who did not believe she was asking his special preference. Audiences of all ages soon loved Emma.

Emma's Sunday

recitals

delighted many

a young man

★ ★ ★ ★ ★ ★

It was at school that she met and befriended Dr. Adrian Ebell, a naturalist, and his lovely wife. When the Ebells decided to tour Europe, they arranged to take Emma along so that she might seriously begin to study for a singing career.

As a final gesture of goodwill before leaving, Emma returned to Austin to perform in a benefit concert. A local miner had lost both feet in an accident and Emma wished to help him. The concert proved to be not only a success for her as a singer but a financial triumph for the injured miner. The concert took in receipts totaling $407, a fine amount for a small-town benefit.

The concert was held in the Austin Methodist Church, and in the *Reese River Reveille* of March 17, 1877 her talents were praised:

" 'The Happy Birdling' is the title of a solo sung by Miss Emma Wixom, and judging from the brightness of the tiers of countenances . . . it seemed to impart a feeling of joyousness to all present. . . . Tremendous applause followed. On reappearing Miss Wixom sang and played "Listen to the Mocking Bird," and Mr. House whistled as the mocking bird behind the curtain. The effect was sublime. . ."

The next day Emma left Austin for New York and Europe. But all was not to go well for the traveling study group. Ebell became very ill; before they reached Hamburg, he died, leaving the party penniless. Mrs. Ebell, fraught with grief and facing instant poverty, returned to America. But not Emma. She had crossed the ocean, and now, full of ambition, she made up her mind to stay as long as she could.

A moment at rest

Even in those days such news traveled fast, so it was not long before her friends in the mining camps heard of the diva's dilemma. They got together and raised enough money for the young woman to com-

97

plete her training. With the additional help of another friend, Emma went to Vienna, where she studied for three and a half years with the famous Mathilde Marchesi.

Under the guidance of this noted voice teacher, Emma eagerly submitted herself to the rigid discipline required of aspiring opera singers. It proved to be the best thing she was to do.

Debut in

London society

★ ★ ★ ★ ★ ★ ★

In three short years Emma made her debut at Her Majesty's Theatre in London. She had by now dropped the name Wixom and had adopted a name suggestive of her background: Emma Nevada. Performing "La Sonnambula," her success was acclaimed world-wide. This prompted one San Francisco newspaper writer to call her "The Sagebrush Linnet."

For several years she appeared in various Italian opera houses and in the Opéra Comique of Paris. Other European engagements followed in France, Italy, and Germany, but even with mounting fame, she remained little changed by success. While returning to England in 1884 to sing "Rose of Sharon," an opera written especially for her, Emma was invited to appear before Queen Victoria. She later wrote to her first music teacher of the occasion. "Her Majesty asked me if I was not an American and I proudly answered 'from California'—and I almost added 'from Mills.' "

That trip was to be significant for another phase of Emma's life, for it also produced a romance. It was here she met Dr. Raymond Palmer. Although he belonged to a medical family long established in Staffordshire, he quickly closed his practice and

98

went on tour in America as Emma's physician, secretary, and companion to the young singer's father.

In the spring of 1885 with the Mapleson Opera Company, Emma started west once more. Her trunks were filled with beautiful gowns, and her musical repertoire bulged with new and old and enduring favorites. Her heart was yearning to be received by her own people. She was not disappointed. The entire state made ready a heartfelt welcome. After all, she was the first California-born singer to attain prominence in the extremely difficult field of European grand opera.

Newspapers hailed her return appearances with flowery words and phrases. One paper went so far as to call her "The California Patti" after Adelina Patti, an international operatic celebrity for nearly two decades. Another newspaper acknowledged her as "a prima donna" and noted that "she will be welcomed with affection, for all have admired her voice immensely."

Newspaper greets her success with discretion

★ ★ ★ ★ ★ ★

The competitive newspapers discreetly commented:

"They say that her upper notes are beautiful, that she has wonderful sustaining power which will hold a note until the audience is gasping for breath, that there is a sympathy in her voice which will make you weep; but to compare her to Patti is simply folly, such as likening a linnet to a nightingale. . . . But Nevada is our home bird, and we shall welcome her with affection, admire her voice immensely for all there is in it, and find excellencies that less loving ears have missed. . . ."

99

Emma had been ill much of the tour, suffering from neuralgia and the extraction of two teeth. Later, a cold and tonsillitis also struck. By the time she reached San Francisco there was some doubt that she would appear. But by the time she reached town her health was better, and it was announced that she would keep all her engagements, "singing at her finest." After her arrival, Colonel Mapleson had her test her voice. The results were printed in the *Alta:* ". . . a peal of glorious, silver-toned melody rang out and filled the halls and corridors of the Montgomery Street side of the fifth floor of the Palace. . . ."

Reception of her appearance at the Grand Opera House on the evening of March 23, 1885 was next morning hailed as "enthusiasm bordering on lunacy." The audience applause was of the type and volume more frequently heard at political rallies than at the opera.

At the end of the first act, bowing to the shouts of "Bravo!" showered upon her, Emma heard someone in the audience cry "Home Sweet Home." With a faltering voice she attempted to sing the first words. The effort failed, and she fled from the stage overcome with emotion. Responding to continued applause, Emma returned on stage and sang the ballad with moistened eyes. The crowd went wild with joy. Emma crowned the conductor with one of her laurel wreaths, and tripped lightly off the stage with the grace of a kitten.

At the end of the second act the enthusiasm had reached such heights that Colonel Mapleson appeared. Bouquets and more bouquets, intended for Emma, grazed his bald head. A long series of gifts were passed over the footlights; all were later carefully described by the press. But the final gift made the biggest impact: a purse of $2000 in five-dollar gold pieces, raised by subscription through the efforts of her former classmates at Mills College. The performance lasted until after 11 o'clock, when the green curtain fell for the last time, hiding the songstress from view, amidst endless shouts of "Bravo! Bravo!"

Her voice was praised by critics and described as "clear, pure, sweet and flexible . . . but never very sonorous." Other writers commented on the ease and confidence with which she sang the more difficult passages of the role of Amina in "La Sonnambula." They also had praise for the second act finale, when her reed-like voice rose over the roar of the chorus and ensemble like a skyrocket. . . ."

Emma Nevada couldn't have given more of herself if she had tried. The city loved her and their admiration came spontaneously. So great was the affection for the young California star that one candy dealer named some caramels after her. Emma responded happily, "They are called 'Nevada creams'. . ."

Rumors of her romance with Dr. Palmer spread with her popularity, and two months later she acknowledged that they were true. The couple would be married in Paris in October.

After her triumphant tour of America, Emma and her entourage returned to Europe. Regarding her approaching marriage she wrote the following letter to her former teacher, Mrs. Mills.

July 21, 1885

My dear Mrs. Mills:

I'm sure you think me a very naughty girl for so long neglecting you, but indeed my life has been such a change of scene since I left you that there has been very little time left me for anything but dress-makers and business letters.

Our trip over the ocean was the same dreadful monotonous journey that it always is—I sick all the way—not being able to put on a dress until the last day. Papa was greatly benefited by the trip and at present has very little sign of paralysis. After spending a day in London we went directly to the country home of Dr. Palmer in Acton, about 20 miles from London. And it was there, dear Mrs. Mills, that Dr. Palmer asked for my hand and was accepted by my dear good father. How can I find words to tell you how happy I am, not only that I am engaged to the best man in all the world but I am to be married to him on October the first on Thursday morning at eleven o'clock in Paris. How I do wish you all could be there. We had at first arranged to have the wedding in June (next) in San Francisco but then we thought it was all nonsense being separated when we might just as well be enjoying life together, for indeed we are very happy and I feel quite sure God always intended us for each other.

Paris is in a state of great excitement over this approaching marriage. You know the Parisians rather claim me as their child—and of course everything I do interests them immensely. We spend our honeymoon in Fontainbleau near Paris and sail for America on the 17th of October on the steamship "Servia." I am engaged by C. A. Chizzola . . . for a five months concert tour all over America to commence the 2nd of November. I preferred concert this season as there are so many places in America that cannot afford an opera and I am an American girl and don't see why the small cities should be slighted when one song might gladden the hearts of thousands. We expect to be in San Francisco about the middle of January and will visit all the largest cities in California and Nevada. . . .

Hoping that you are well and taking a good rest during the summer months, I am as always your loving child and ever grateful pupil.

Emma Nevada

The wedding was a brilliant event, preceded by a public showing of the bride's trousseau. The bridal party went first to the British Embassy and the American Legation for civil ceremonies, then to the Church of the English Passionists, where Emma had taken her first Catholic communion a year and a half earlier. The church glowed with scarlet and gold hangings and the air was fragrant with the scent of flowers. Glowing with happiness, Emma came in on the arm of her father. On her head was a wreath of fresh orange blossoms, from which a veil fell the full length of the train of her gown, which was of white velvet. It, too, was edged with fresh orange blossoms.

Trousseau on public display

✴ ✴ ✴ ✴ ✴ ✴

103

Nevada Theatre program

NEVADA THEATRE
Monday Evening, March 31, 1902

THE WORLD-FAMED SINGER,

Mme. Emma
NEVADA

Assisted by the Eminent Pianist
and Composer,

Leon Moreau

PROGRAM

PART I

1. LEON MOREAU
   (a) Nocturne............ ....Liszt
   (b) Waltz ....,.... ... ...Moszkowski

2. MADAME NEVADA.
   (a) Song of the Mysoli....... ....David
       From the Pearl of Brazil.
   (b) Air ....Selected

3. LEON MOREAU.
   (a) Dans la Nuit ....Leon Moreau
   (b) Chanson Dansee ......,...Leon Moreau

4. MADAME NEVADA.
   (a) Ave Maria..... ....Schubert
   (b) Villanelle..... ....Dell'Acqua

PART II

1. MADAME NEVADA.
   (a) A Tale of Two Apples .....Laura Collins
   (b) The Sleepy Little Sister.....Schlesinger
   (c) You and I.... ....Liza Lehmann

2. LEON MOREAU.
   (a) The Spinning Wheel...........J. Raff
   (b) Rhapsodie Hongroise, No. 12.....Liszt

3. MADAME NEVADA.
   Selections.......... ....

This programme subject to alteration without notice.

UNION AND HERALD PRINT

After the ceremony, the couple received felicitations that were telegraphed from all over Europe. Their best man, Tommaso Salvini, the great tragedian, slipped a handsome diamond bracelet over the bride's wrist. Hidden from many guests by a six-foot high wedding cake imported from London, Emma rang a silver bell whenever she wanted to call atten-

104

tion to a particularly eloquent speech or toast. Often she darted from her seat to kiss the speaker on the cheek and present him with a sugar flower.

Afterward the bride and groom left for St. Germain, and within a few days sailed for New York and the winter concert season. The following year, their only child, Mignon, was born in Paris.

Although Emma sang extensively at La Scala, Covent Garden, the Royal Opera of Madrid, and other great European houses, she returned to America only three more times, to appear with the Hinrichs Opera Company in Philadelphia in the season of 1895–96 and to make long concert tours to the West in 1900 and 1902.

Emma died quietly in June 1940 in London during a German bombing raid. Her husband, Dr. Palmer, had passed away four years earlier. Her daughter Mignon also became a noted opera singer. Trained entirely by her mother, she sang often in Lisbon, Milan, London, Paris, and other European cities. And like her mother, she ended her career as a teacher of singing.

Emma had many high points in her life, and perhaps one worth recalling involved a Shoshone Indian chief. When she crossed the high Toiyabe Range of the Sierra Nevada, Shoshone children were among those waiting to greet her. Their chief, Toi Toi, stepped forward and greeted the prima soprano, bridging the distance between their two worlds and reaching the woman's heart. To his people, Chief Toi Toi told her, the great Emma Nevada was "the Songbird of the Mountains."

7

CASSIE HILL

WIFE, MOTHER, TELEGRAPHER, WELLS FARGO AGENT

y dear sister:

Last Tuesday we had one of the grandest birthday parties our home has yet to have. Of course the beautifully decorated cake, with its pink and yellow roses reminiscent of old Roseville was special, the punch extra tangy, the guests most enjoyable. But it was the birthday girl who was spectacular. Not that she is a girl—by no means. But her qualities, tiny build, twinkling eyes the color of ripening wheat, and a smile that reveals a lust for living, remind one of youth. That alone, I would imagine, contributed to Cassie Hill's 100th year on this great earth. Yes, I did say 100, and years full of abundant living, sensitivity and, I rather guess, a bit of sensationalism. She was once a Wells Fargo agent during the last century, a period when most women either took care of their large families or taught school. But Cassie wasn't a single woman without responsibilities, or one who had a man around to help with bringing up a brood of five. For a time Cassie had both. But she also had another career.

In the misty sienna glow of the old Roseville railroad depot, with its wood-burning potbelly stove, iron scales, and straight-back chairs, Cassie took meticulous care of in and outgoing express, both human and otherwise, noting destination, weight, departure time, and content of packages to be shipped. Wearing the familiar green visor pulled down over her brown hair, white gauzy sleeves cuffed at the elbows, long skirts brushing the wood-planked floors, she treated each traveler with friend-liness and respect.

"I'm looking for the Wells Fargo man," a burly, dusty cowboy asked, slinging his grips onto the oak counter. He dropped a smoke on the floor, killing the fire with the toe of well-worn boots.

Getting up from the rolltop desk, Cassie pushed back the visor and smiled. "You're looking at her."

"You're the Wells Fargo agent?" He looked sur-prised.

"Sure am. What can I do for you?"

For a moment the cowboy was stunned, speech-less. Three children darted into the room, one carry-ing firewood for the hungry stove, the oldest boy dragging a box of peaches he was going to sell to train customers, and a small girl kicking at a crate to make it move. Cassie paid little attention to her clamoring children. By now she was used to having them mix with the business of operating a Wells Fargo station.

Finally the cowboy recovered from his initial shock; he shrugged his shoulders and proceeded to tell Cassie what he wanted shipped back East. "I reckon you can count alright. I've got two grips and this box. Want them to go to my mother in Phila-delphia. Does your train go there?"

"Sure will." Cassie took the pencil from behind her ear and got out an order form.

Cassie Tomer Hill was born into a struggling Iowa family in August of 1854. Ma and Pa Tomer had six children and country living for them was difficult at best. After hearing all those exciting tales about

I reckon you can count, *the cowboy conceded*

the California Gold Rush, with creeks lined with precious ore ready for the picking, Pa Tomer must have decided he could do no worse out West. So he and Ma Tomer packed up all six children, and with their meager belongings, joined a train of some seventy-five covered wagons that were headed for California. Cassie was 2 years old at this time. It must have been pretty hard for that poor mother and all those kids in one wagon, all wishing they were already in the promised land. But then, it was determined folk such as the Tomers who built much of the great state of California. Each child had one toy, perhaps a cloth doll or a carved animal, to help idle away the time as they bounced along in the wagon. The weather changed from extreme cold to desert heat, depending on the altitude. Many fellow travelers became ill, and those who died were buried along side the trail, with a fallen tree for a headstone. Hardship was commonplace.

The Tomer family traveled for five months and ten days to the Nevada territory, where they first settled. But living wasn't any easier there, and after four years of trying to satisfy the growing family's needs, Pa Tomer moved on, this time settling on a small ranch near Woodland, California. Northwest of Sacramento, Woodland was once a rolling, grassy prairie dotted with wide gangling oaks, brilliant California poppies, and waves of wild bush lupine and native weeds. In the summer the air was dry and lazy and warm winds danced across the rangelands. Jackrabbits and grey squirrels scurried easily between the woody coverings, and doves and noisy black crows abounded. The Tomer children must have had great fun in those vast and tranquil fields.

Woodland is a short distance from Roseville, where Cassie was to eventually settle and become somewhat of a celebrity. In those days wild roses mingled with the other native flora, and this contributed to the naming of this community, which became the home of an enormous railroad roundhouse owned by Southern Pacific Railroad. When Cassie was 22 years old she married George W. Hill. His family had come to California in the 1850s by way of Panama, settling first at Michigan Bluff and later in Auburn. Young Hill worked for the railroad, and shortly after his marriage to Cassie the newlyweds moved to Hanford, where he served as agent and telegrapher. With a family of her own, Cassie spent her days cooking and sewing for the children. She had always loved Roseville, and so when her husband was transferred there in 1881, her dreams must have been satisfied.

"I'm sorry we have to make our home in the depot," the tall, slightly built Hill told his young wife, "with the continuous clamor of trains and people. But it's the best I can manage right now. Perhaps later we can have our own home and a nice big yard."

Cassie smiled brightly. "It's fine with me, George. We're all together here and I do so love Roseville. It's such a bustling community."

Already Roseville was becoming an extensive shipping and trading center, having been the favored location for the railroad junction in the heart of southern Placer County's rich agricultural region. With an eye to the future, pioneer O. D. Lombard in August of 1864 drew up plans for a new city, to be called Roseville.

But the existing town was already very nice. Recently planted orchards and newly constructed farms laced the surrounding countryside and dotted the prairie. To the eastward, the lofty, lavender Sierra foothills etched the horizon. It was no wonder that Cassie loved Roseville so much.

The first building to be erected in Roseville Junction, as it was then called, was the freight depot, built and operated by Cyrus W. Taylor. It was here that George Hill worked, and the family lived in the upper end of the elongated structure. For a time it was the busiest spot in town, with trains and people arriving and leaving daily.

Depot in Roseville, California

But as cruel fate would have it, Cassie's dear husband died after only a few years at his job. She was left with five small children to rear in a railroad depot. The future was uncertain at best. Yet Cassie had that rich pioneer blood flowing in her veins, and she quickly asked to take over her husband's job. There was naturally some doubt expressed by the male members of the town.

"But she's so young, and with all the children," one townsman said. "How can she run an express depot?"

"And the telegraph—she doesn't know anything about that," another said.

"I know how to tap out the telegraph," Cassie said, speaking up with determination. "I've been helping George these past years. Let me try. I know I can do a fine job."

"Well, I don't know," one man said. "You'd work long hours, daybreak to nighttime."

But they also realized Cassie's desperate situation, and it was known that several other women had worked for Wells Fargo at other locations. Therefore, it was duly decided that they would try her out. When Wells Fargo agreed, Cassie took over her husband's job.

Whatever doubts the residents of Roseville had about Cassie were soon quelled by her performance. The impressive Wells Fargo & Company certificate that hung in her office must have given her pride. It carefully spelled out her duties, noting that Mrs. C. Hill was appointed as agent of Wells Fargo &

Cassie Hill's Wells Fargo certificate

Company's express at Roseville on May 14, 1884. In those days, women held few jobs of responsibility.

How Wells Fargo & Company became part of the Southern Pacific Railroad in Roseville is also an interesting piece of California history, and it set the background for Cassie's life story. When the two great railroad lines joined at Promontory Point in 1869, stagecoaching was for all intents and purposes over. The romantic, rough mode of travel had given way to a better one. But would Wells Fargo & Company get the contract to handle express aboard the new steam-driven coaches, replacing their horse-drawn Concords? Since the stagecoach–banking

113

firm had not been too friendly with the railroads, a future alliance was questionable. Then, in September of 1869, the Central Pacific Railroad granted the Pacific Express Company the exclusive privilege of handling express over its new tracks. Such a situation seemed ruinous to Wells Fargo, and officers of the company lost no time in seeking arrangements with their competitors. A joint meeting of directors of both companies was held at Omaha on October 4. Representing Wells Fargo were the powerful William G. Fargo, Charles Fargo, and A. H. Barney.

At this momentous conference Wells Fargo & Company was given, for a consideration of $5,000,000, the privilege of handling express over the Central Pacific, which later became the Southern Pacific Railroad.

High financing

saved

Wells Fargo

★ ★ ★ ★ ★ ★

A stormy meeting of Wells Fargo stockholders followed on November 25th to discuss how to raise the necessary funds to conclude the transaction. It appears that this huge sum of money was raised by increasing the capital stock of the company from $10 million to $15 million. At the time the price paid seemed like financial highjacking, but it proved later to be sound banking indeed. For had Wells Fargo not made this investment, its express service might well have gone the way of its stagecoach line.

Cassie Hill was soon doing an extraordinary job for the company, both as express agent and as one of the first women telegraphers.

There is in the history room of Wells Fargo &

114

Company the following personal memoir written about another Wells Fargo agent, also a woman. It describes a typical day for the express agent.

"She took the job as agent following the death of her husband to support herself and her son. She would rise at 4 a.m. She always kept the outside door of her bedroom open to permit the chill night air to enter. This was the way, she felt, to keep one's self strong and vigorous. She would take a sponge bath with cold water, again to remain vigorous, and then rub herself with a coarse Turkish towel till warmth returned. Then, following the style of the day, she would put on layer after layer of clothing. She would wrap herself in a shawl and set out for the agency office which was also the town's Post Office.

"The first thing she had to do was build a fire in the stove, then sort and stamp letters and unlock the heavy iron safe where gold and other valuables were stored. Following the arrival of the morning stage, she went back home for breakfast and then devoted an hour or so to tutoring the school children in spelling.

"Then it was back to the office again, which she had to sweep out, bring in wood for the fire, bring her books up to date, and write her reports. She remained in the agency until the evening stage arrived, usually around 8 p.m. So her working day for Wells Fargo and Uncle Sam ran from 4 a.m. to 8 p.m."

At the time of Cassie's appointment, there was a saloon run by John Louis Buien at one end of the depot. The depot itself occupied the central portion of the long building, and Cassie and her family continued to live in the upper end.

Forrest Hill, one of Cassie's five children, later recalled a particular job he had while the family lived there. As a small boy he had made a deal with a certain Tom Royer, whose big house and vast grounds were on Vernon Street, where the Bank of America building currently sits. He would sell grapes and other fruits from the Royer ranch to passengers on the trains and split the profits fifty-fifty. Hill remembered that this deal proved to be very lucrative.

All the Hill children had various small jobs while they were growing up, and by all accounts Cassie managed the family resources quite well. She continued to make her home in the depot until 1907, when a new building was completed below the railroad "Y," and the old building was dismantled. Part of it was subsequently moved to Atlantic Street, where it was used as a saloon.

At the time the old depot was destroyed, Cassie retired. She wrote a poem to commemorate its memory.

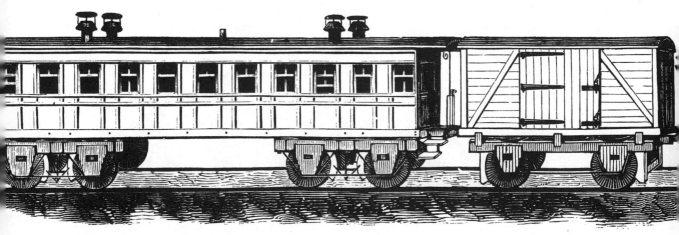

After retirement, she invested her savings in the Cassie Hill building on Lincoln Street, maintaining a home on the second floor. The ground floor was then a jewelry store. In 1941 the building was purchased by John Leles, who operated a butcher shop and grocery store. Today this part of the building is occupied by a bar.

Cassie continued to reside in Roseville until 1950, when the infirmities of old age compelled her to enter a rest home. In the year 1954 she celebrated her 100th birthday.

Cassie Hill brought up five fine children, contributed a large share to the business growth of Roseville, and left a pioneer legacy of the historic Wells Fargo era. Quite a distinction for a young woman from Iowa.

"THE OLD DEPOT"

The old home is not what it used to be
The thoughts lurk near me still;
'Tis but the fleeting past I see
Where all is calm and still.

Thirty years have past since first
I trod its threshold dear to me,
and now 'tis but a dream of yore,
The old home I cannot see.

My children, from their infancy,
No other home they knew;
And now how sad for them to see
The old go for the new.

Henry too has left me
Pastures new to find
But ponders o'er the past to see
And dreams of things unkind.

And wonders why this change is made.
The new town "is to be,"
But claims 'tis nothing more than this—
The cruel Espee.

My greatest comfort now
Is little Hillie dear
With eyes of thoughtful earnestness
And mind of gentle cheer.

The food for grave inquiring speech
He everywhere doth find
And asks me o'er and o'er again
Why were we left behind.

No more will I the clatter hear
Of instruments at my door;
And wonder why the trains
Don't stop as they did in days of yore.

Goodbye Espee, I'll not forget you
Nor all the kindness you have shown;
You have sheltered me from girlhood.
I for you, with age have grown.

And now I am to leave you
I scarcely know what to do;
And everytime I think of it,
It makes me think of you.

Cassie Hill

8

ELEANOR WEBBER

Detail of photograph. Courtesy of Amon Carter Museum, Fort Worth

SHE WANTED A HUSBAND. HE WANTED GOLD!

Gold was still being discovered and mined in California as late as the 1870s, but its abundance and easy recovery were waning. Nevertheless, thousands of hopeful people were still braving the hazardous elements and coming west. Eleanor Webber arrived in 1873. A rather plain-appearing girl of proud parentage with a determined streak in her young mind, she also sought her fortune. But unlike the others, she did not come for gold. She had only one burning reason, and that was to get married.

Arrangements had been made in the East, and while Eleanor had never seen her prospective spouse, friends who had known the tall and handsome man assured her she was making the right choice. Several letters of courtship passed through the mail between the prospective bride and bridegroom, and in the early spring, Eleanor Webber set out for California with a beautiful trousseau of silk and satin. She was confident of her future. Love would triumph over all.

Taking the recently completed railroad across the great western frontier, Eleanor, tired but happy, alighted at the town of Colfax. From there she would board a large Concord stagecoach for the short journey to Grass Valley and her matrimonial union.

The July afternoon was warm, the sky a cornflower blue, and the foothills tinged with summer green. Eleanor's heart was pounding excitedly. How long she had waited for this moment—to be a married woman.

The least attractive of the Webber children, Eleanor tried extra hard at being friendly and charming. She loved to clean house, crochet, and read. In the spring months she was the first to gather wildflowers in the woods, bringing home armfuls to grace the china vases in the parlor. And she also had a natural talent for writing verse.

Eleanor also had large brown eyes. When she was younger, several naughty neighbor boys had called her "owl eyes," but as she grew up and her face filled out, the eyes looked better. They had always sparkled with innocence, never revealing the hurt she sometimes felt. After all, being plain had cost her having beaus, and that was what she had dreamed of all those years growing up. But now her luck had changed. The time to blossom had come. Eleanor was going to marry a handsome and adventurous prospector who, according to his letters, was doing quite well in the West as a mine superintendent. Her heart skipped once more as she approached the waiting coach, the last lap of her journey.

"Welcome aboard, Miss." Wells Fargo agent William B. Story extended his hand to assist Eleanor. "Going to be a fine trip this afternoon. Not too long a ride."

"Thank you," Eleanor replied politely. "I will be so pleased to finally reach my destination. It seems I have been traveling forever." Despite the arduous journey, the thought of her impending marriage made her prettier than ever, giving her a certain sparkle.

"Yes, ma'am," Story said, smiling. He rubbed his hands down the sides of his jeans, aware that they were not very clean. After all, this was a real lady, and there were still not too many of them out here. "You staying in Grass Valley?" he asked.

Eleanor lowered her eyelids, glancing at a spot on the toe of her tiny leather shoes. "I'm getting married," she said, her long skirts rustling.

"Ah, a bride," he said. "I thought maybe so. Well, it's good news for some lucky man. Just what this country needs—pretty wives."

Eleanor continued to smile; then, noticing the size of the coach, she asked where she should sit.

"Why, take the inside seat in the rear. It's cushioned and extra soft." Story winked. "Besides, it's the richest and most expensive."

Eleanor frowned and shook her brown curls. "I'm sorry, I don't know what you mean."

"Oh, just a joke, Miss. The seats are all comfortable. But that one happens to be covering the built-in iron strongbox, where we keep the gold. Today it contains almost $8,000. We've carried more, back aways. But this ain't so bad either."

"Oh," Eleanor remarked, smoothing down her long skirts. "Then I shall sit upon it. Besides, I wouldn't want to get dusty by the window."

"Well, have a good trip, and best of luck."

"Thank you," Eleanor said properly.

"So you've come out West to meet your new husband," a passenger said loudly. E. Black Ryan, an Irish attorney, was next to climb aboard the stage. Grinning and smelling of Irish whiskey, he stretched out his hand. "A lovely lass indeed to keep us company during this short but discomforting ride."

Her eyelids

lowered,

I'm getting

married

★ ★ ★ ★ ★ ★

Eleanor acknowledged the new passenger, and after several minutes, a total of eleven men got on. Some were miners returning to the fields, others were merchants. Bob Scott, the driver, appeared, pulling on leather gloves and adjusting his wide-brimmed hat. "Grass Valley it be," he shouted.

The fresh team broke into a gallop, red dust flying about the huge wooden wheels. Eleanor caught at her bonnet and choked with surprise. Certainly it wasn't at all like the train ride. Soon the stagecoach was rolling down the curving road to the Bear River. A thick screen of pines and cedars shielded the mountains from view. Inside, the passengers were enjoying the merriment of Ryan who, after getting comfortable by a window, had broken into a repertoire of Irish songs. His lovely tenor voice delighted all. Eleanor, with thoughts of wedded bliss bracing her mind, consented to join in also. Her voice was true and sweet.

Beyond the Bear River, the pace slowed for the long climb up the manzanita-covered slopes. The horses snorted and bobbed their heads. The singing inside continued despite the heat and dust, and Ryan passed his bottle to the other men.

The stage had reached the lower acres of Sheet's Ranch, only five miles from the Grass Valley station, when four masked men stepped into the road. Seeing the road blocked, the driver quickly hauled back on the reins and slammed the brake with his foot. The team skidded and reared, tossing several of the passengers onto the floor.

"By golly, if it isn't a holdup," Ryan bellowed in his rich tenor.

Eleanor tried to look outside the coach, but the dust and the other passengers blocked her view. But she did hear the highwaymen yell for all the passengers to climb out.

"What does this mean?" she asked.

"Never you worry, little lady," Ryan said, taking her arm. "Soon as they get what they want we'll be on our way again."

Outside the coach, Eleanor immediately saw the four double-barreled shotguns, aimed at the driver. Scott was silent, keenly aware of what could happen if the wrong moves were made.

"Everyone out," the bandit leader shouted, "and unhitch the team."

"What do you want?" the driver asked, although it was all too certain what they wanted.

"The strong box with the gold," came the answer.

"But it's on the other stage," Scott replied, attempting to thwart the robbery.

"You know better than that," the leader shouted. "Everyone out. It's right here. You know there aren't two coaches running on Sunday."

Eleanor's legs were cramped anyway, and she shook her shoulders, trying to regain her natural good posture. Despite the threatening situation she did not feel frightened. Instead, she was very curious about these men whose faces were covered by masks.

The leader pointed to two of his men. They leveled their shotguns, knowing what to do next. "Over there," one shouted, using his gun to point out a clearing some thirty yards down the road. "Get over there and sit down, cross-legged, in a row." Eleanor,

Over there,

one shouted,

using his gun

★ ★ ★ ★ ★ ★ ★

20 MILES TO
DEADWOOD LY

$1000
His N t Co t f
Dead o live

Detail of photograph. Courtesy of Amon Carter Museum, Fort Worth

however, was allowed to remain standing, so as not to dirty her skirts.

Meanwhile, the leader and one of his men had quickly uncovered the iron strongbox, attacking it with a miner's pick. They broke the outer lock, but were stopped from stripping it of its contents by a second padlock.

"Going to take more than this pick," one masked man said to the leader.

"Then get the blasting powder."

A third man produced a canister of powder and some fuse. Suddenly Eleanor realized what was happening and nervously spoke up. "Gentlemen," she said. "It is evident that you are going to use powder to blow open the safe. My trunk, which is on the deck of the stage, will in all probability be blown to pieces. It contains all that I own in this world. And while its destruction will not benefit you in the least, it will be an irreplaceable loss to me. Please, I beg you, take it down first."

The masked bandit leader gallantly reassured her. "Certainly, Miss, with the greatest pleasure." Setting the canister down, he climbed up onto the deck of the stagecoach and carefully slid the trunk down over the boot to his waiting companion. The other masked man carefully carried it to safety. As the leader hefted the trunk, the wind tugged at his mask and Eleanor momentarily had a glimpse of the man's face. She smiled thinly, saying "Thank you."

Two men resumed tamping powder around the lock. After there was a sufficient amount inserted, they attached a long fuse and lit it cautiously.

Rejoining the rest of the gang and the passengers seated on the ground, they waited quietly, flinching in anticipation of the explosion. There was no blast, however. After a full minute, the impatient leader walked up to the strongbox to see what had gone wrong. He glanced inside the coach and then jerked around, taking off at a dead run. The warning hiss of the burning fuse was swallowed up by a brilliant flash of fire and a great roar, which echoed off the immovable Sierras.

Quickly the bandits moved in, barely waiting for the smoke to clear. The ruptured strongbox left a gaping hole in the rear of the stage, and its valuable contents were scattered over the roadway.

"Hurry up, boys," the leader shouted, "before someone down the road figures out what caused the explosion." He tossed Eleanor's trunk back into the shattered stage, and waved at the group of bewildered passengers to board. "Hitch up and get moving," he said to the driver.

Scott gathered his frightened passengers on board the damaged coach. The top of the strongbox, now bent double, had blown through the roof, and portions of the lock were embedded in the fine woodwork. The coach lining was shredded and light filtered in from many spots.

Fortunately, Scott found the running gear undamaged. He quickly hitched up the team and whipped at the air. Soon the ironshod hooves were moving across the road, the bandits having already disappeared into the tangled growth of the darkening mountains.

In a short time the coach arrived at Grass Valley, and the driver then made an unscheduled stop at the address Eleanor had given him in Colfax. She alighted with her trunk in front of a small cottage on the outskirts of town. Welcoming light gleamed onto the front porch; the door stood open awaiting Eleanor.

A woman came out of the house and greeted the young bride. "You must be Eleanor Webber. We've been waiting for you." She put her arm about Eleanor's waist and the two went inside the cottage.

Eleanor broke

into sobs

★ ★ ★ ★ ★ ★

Eleanor looked about, and seeing they were alone, broke into sobs. "I thought he would be here to meet me."

"Louis will be here shortly," the woman said, attempting to relieve the girl's anguish. "He was called out on an emergency."

"But I traveled so far and the journey was not easy."

"Never you mind. He'll be back any time now and all will be well. Here, let me take your bag while you bathe. Then we'll have some supper. You'll feel better then."

"I suppose you're right. I'm very tired and dirty."

An hour or so later, having washed and rested and eaten a hot meal, Eleanor was feeling better. The excitement that earlier had caused her heart to quicken had returned and she awaited eagerly for her husband-to-be, Louis Dreibelbis, to arrive. After what seemed like hours, the woman announced that the bridegroom was here and the wedding would take place shortly.

Eleanor had already unpacked her wedding

gown, shaking out the wrinkles and hanging it by a window to freshen. Now she put it on. Catching sight of herself in the long mirror standing in the corner, she twirled about. "Oh, my!" she said aloud. "I do indeed look pretty." She happily entered the living room.

The woman led her to a corner of the room, where a clergyman and a witness were sitting. The preacher got up abruptly. "Right here, young lady," he said, taking her by the arm. Eleanor looked about, catching sight of the tall, strikingly handsome man standing off to one side, his face partially shaded by a large bouquet of flowers. The preacher continued to busy himself, getting everyone in their correct positions for the wedding ceremony.

Louis' voice sounded strangely familiar when he greeted Eleanor. And for some reason, she guessed shyness, he averted his face. He did not embrace her either, as she had secretly hoped he might.

Eleanor demurely bowed her head as the preacher began the ceremony. The only thing missing was her family. If only they could be here to share this wonderful event with her. At the final moment, all her past fears about being plain were dispelled. To Eleanor Webber, and no doubt to everyone else present, she was the loveliest creature alive. Quietly she answered, "I do."

"Then I now pronounce you man and wife," the preacher concluded. "Louis, you may kiss the bride."

The smiling bridegroom reached down, bending his large body toward her. The light of the kerosene lamp shone directly on his face.

131

"Oh, no!" Eleanor shrieked. "It's you!"

The young man straightened, somewhat embarrassed, and backed away from his new bride.

"How dare you!" she continued, tearing herself from his arms. Turning quickly, she ran from the room, her wedding gown brushing the furniture as she fled. Eleanor had recognized Louis Dreibelbis, her new husband, as the leader of the highwaymen who had earlier robbed the stagecoach.

Dreibelbis, in an equal panic, rushed from the cottage.

To the bewilderment of the preacher and the witnesses, Eleanor locked herself in the bedroom, refusing to come out. Needless to say, that night she cried herself into a fitful slumber.

The next morning she was up bright and early. "Please," she said to her hostess, "I must return home."

The woman shook her head, feeling sad for the young woman who had traveled so far for such a wedding. "Perhaps you were wrong," she said.

"No, I knew him all right. Besides, if he wasn't the same man, why did he run off?"

The woman could not answer that. It was a few moments before Eleanor could speak.

"Now," she said finally, her composure returning, "I shall book passage on the next stage."

Her shoulders straight, her eyes red with humiliation and heartbreak, Eleanor left Grass Valley forever.

The day after the robbery, Wells Fargo detective Jim Hume was already on the trail of the Dreibelbis gang. He arrested Charles Thompson, an accomplice in the crime, who immediately told all. Not only had they robbed the Colfax stage, they had also robbed the Downieville stage earlier.

The following month, Hume got another tip. This time it was reported that a man fitting the description of the stage robber was living in a hotel in Coloma. He was "well-fixed," said the informant, but always sad. He bought shoes for some of the barefoot youngsters of the town, and had lately taken to drowning his sorrows in the nearest saloon.

The man, now calling himself Walker, had given his landlady a small gold bar and several hundred dollars for safekeeping. He told her that he had been a mine superintendent at the St. Patrick Mine in Placer County and had left well-fixed.

The detective checked with the mine and, finding no record of a superintendent named Walker, he left immediately for Coloma. He persuaded the landlady to show him the gold bar and the other coins. He discovered that many of the gold coins were bent and smoke-blackened. Obviously they were the survivors of a recent explosion. Hume easily found Walker in a saloon. But Walker was so badly disturbed that the detective placed him in the care of a local doctor before sending him to jail.

After he recovered, Hume questioned him, and learned that he was Louis Dreibelbis, the bridegroom of Eleanor Webber. He had been well educated in the Midwest and had come to California to seek his fortune. Failing to do this, he had drifted into a life of robbing stagecoaches.

"If I give you a full confession, will you help me?" he asked the detective.

"I can promise you nothing," Hume replied. "But we will be fair."

"Yes, I suppose you will be. And I should have known better anyway. Robbery was no solution."

Louis told him about the crimes and mentioned the names of the others involved. The detective telegraphed the Grass Valley sheriff. Together they sought out the other four accomplices: a saloon-keeper, a miner, and two ne'er-do-wells. They went directly to the mine to find the suspected miner, Nat Stover. The superintendent found it hard to believe, stating, "Why, Nat is the most dependable man I have."

"We just want to question him," Hume pushed, "and take a look around his cabin."

"Okay, but I think you have made a mistake." The superintendent went outside and pointed up the hillside. "He lives up there with some gal."

Together, Hume and the superintendent moved toward the darkened cabin. When the door finally opened, a large, savage dog broke into fierce barking, but Nat Stover pulled him back.

"Get your shirt on," Hume told Stover. "We're taking you in for stage robbery."

Stover was silent but his girlfriend leaped out of bed and ran toward Nat, flinging her arms about him. "You can't arrest him. He's done nothing wrong."

Hume, ignoring the young woman, went over to the bed, shaking out the pillows and tossing the blankets back. "So," he said, "you're only a miner. Then why do you have this loaded six-shooter?"

The superintendent stood back, surprised at this

turn of events. The Grass Valley sheriff appeared and Nat Stover was taken down the hill, handcuffed to the wagon, and led off to jail. Like Louis, he talked, telling the detective that the saloonkeeper's share of the money was buried under a log in a nearby ravine.

The next day Stover took him to the location, but the officers found that the treasure was already gone. Being a diligent detective, Hume and the sheriff went to the saloonkeeper and convinced him it was all over. They had enough evidence from the other two to convict him also. In short order three of the four robbers were behind bars. The fourth man was later traced to Virginia City, arrested, and returned to California to stand trial. In the end all four men went to prison.

But what of the wayward bridegroom, Louis Dreibelbis? According to the newspaper, "He was the prettiest, most obliging witness ever put on the stand." And the fact that he had told all, revealing names and places, secured him his freedom.

"Well, I hope you learned your lesson," Detective Hume said to Dreibelbis. "Robbing stagecoaches is no way to make a living."

Louis nodded his head sadly. "It cost me a lot," he said. "Including the nicest girl I'll ever know — my wife."

Like thousands of others who came to California during the Gold Rush era to seek their fortunes, Eleanor Webber and Louis Dreibelbis were not successful. Eleanor returned to her home a bit wiser, perhaps, but brokenhearted. As for Louis, unlike other stagecoach robbers, his life of crime was short-lived and his punishment was the ache of his own heart.

Hiding place found — but gold chest gone

☆ ☆ ☆ ☆ ☆ ☆

135

DONALDINA CAMERON

THE MISSIONARY FRIEND OF CHINESE SLAVE GIRLS

It was a little past midnight when an urgent knock was heard on the mission door. A chilly mist had cloaked the city of San Francisco earlier in the day. There were no stars visible and the moon had not shown itself all week. Most people were sleeping, totally uninterested in the tawdry happenings of the waterfront and of squalid Chinatown. But not Donaldina Cameron, a superintendent of the Presbyterian Mission. She was still sitting at her desk, meticulously writing notes to her staff, directing the school's daily activities. This remarkable woman was used to late-night callers, and the ominous knock hardly disturbed her.

"Who is it?" Miss Cameron asked, standing up and leaving the glow of the oil lamp atop her cluttered desk.

"Please, Miss Cameron," the Chinese servant boy said, his breath coming in short gasps, "let me in."

Dressed in a traditional Chinese embroidered night robe, her manner gentle, Donaldina unlatched the large doors. Brushing back wiry white hair, her good Scottish face and spirited dark eyes flashed a welcome. "Come in quickly, Chiang. It is damp and cold outside."

The slightly built Oriental, his back bowed from carrying heavy parcels, looked over his shoulder, peering into the dark mists of the night, and padded hastily inside. "They mustn't see me," he said. He was visibly frightened and knew all too well what would happen if the Tongs caught him coming to the mission for help. For if the notorious Chinese enforcers had one single outstanding enemy other than those of their own criminal kind, it was the missionary lady, Donaldina Cameron. They knew too well the authority and near-idolization she commanded among their own race. They also were aware that once she had given sanctuary to a Chinese slave girl, they had little hope in getting her back, which meant losing money. Sometimes such a loss was substantial.

"Now, Chiang," Donaldina said, her voice calm, "let me fix you some warm tea and you can tell me what's the trouble."

The boy bowed again, stuffing his hands inside his quilted jacket. "No tea, Miss. I must hurry. I'll tell you and leave."

"But surely you need something warm in your stomach."

"No. Not now. Perhaps later."

Donaldina knew and understood her young friend's desperation, and so asked him to explain what had happened to cause him such anxiety.

"A sailing ship, Moon of Canton, arrived at noon today. I see a pretty Chinese girl, about 14 years old, being taken off. I follow and see that she is taken to Tong's basement, where bidding is going on. Poor creature. Tears were coming down her thin cheeks, and her black hair was all messy. But she bring good price: $3,000. Oh, Miss Cameron, you must help Kum Lee, that's her name. She is not the kind of girl for Lotus house."

"Do you know where she is now?"

The boy nodded his head. "She is in tenement in Chinatown. Wicked lady Ah Toy keeps her until tomorrow, when she goes to Lotus house."

"Then we must act fast." Donaldina went back to her desk to write down the location. She knew too well the life of a child bought at auction. It would be one of degradation and near-enslavement, and if the girl was lucky she would be just strong enough to survive some hideous disease. But usually they were undernourished and sickly when they arrrived in San Francisco, and such a life would only make matters worse. Some of the girls had been known to commit suicide; others disappeared completely, and no one ever knew if they killed themselves or were murdered.

But Donaldina Cameron was not new to the methods of the hateful Tongs. She had saved many a girl from their hands, gaining the respect and admiration of the San Francisco police department and certain government leaders, who sincerely believed that she was a chief means of battling the yellow-slave traffic that plagued the city.

She worked quickly and with the diligence of a soldier. Each possible move of the crafty Tongs had to be anticipated and frustrated in a simple rescue from one den to another. More often, however, they first had to search for the girl in the haunts of the highbinders, in the very heart of wickedness, and then wrench her from those who owned her. Then, and only then, would she be free to determine her own future.

Girls faced a life of degradation

★ ★ ★ ★ ★ ★ ★

139

After taking down the location of the latest hide-out, Miss Cameron motioned to the boy, "Now go on your way. And thank you for coming. The Lord surely blesses you and knows of your courage."

By daybreak, Donaldina had received the services of two San Francisco policemen, and with two Chinese girls, themselves rescued slaves, the party had quietly begun an earnest search of the dark Chinatown alley where the abducted girl was being held. On either side of the street were dilapidated brick buildings with many rooms and occupants. Vice was undertaken on the upper floors in a maze of dirty rooms.

The choking mist had given way to windless rain, and the sky was now grey instead of black. Smoke curled about the many tenements, and the pungent scents of herbs and fowl cut the musky morning odors. Chinatown was already awakening, but the sight of policemen and Donaldina Cameron kept the residents behind locked doors. The exploits of this woman were well known here, as were the retaliations of the nearby Tongs.

"This is the one," Miss Cameron finally said, pausing in front of a narrow dark stairway leading to the suspected room. They ascended until they reached the upper story, then Donaldina put her finger to her lips. The police and the two Chinese girls came closer. "We will part here. The girls know what to do from here on in."

Girl in holiday attire ☞

"Are you sure, Miss Cameron?" one officer asked.

"Indeed I am. I have learned to depend on their alert intuition. They will climb to the roof to keep watch while we turn and knock on this door."

The two tiny girls disappeared, their black almond eyes intent on their job, their feet softly but quickly ascending the steps. Miss Cameron and the police stiffened, then knocked forcibly on the door to one of the apartments.

In the outer door of the entrance a slot-panel went back. The American missionary was instantly recognized. Almost at once a frenzy of electric bells warned the chain of tenements that a rescue was in progress.

"We've been exposed," one officer said, using his club to force open the double barricade. "The girl has been removed!"

"No, no," Donaldina exclaimed confidently. "We must pursue them at all speed till we find her!"

"Yes, ma'am," the other officer barked, his big shoulders forcing the doors apart. The light sound of feet echoed down the dim passageway, Miss Cameron and the two officers in close pursuit.

Down the narrow winding hall they went, brushing against the walls, the Irish policeman cursing the low ceiling.

"Now, now, Officer Kelly, a little patience is a virtue. And do be as quiet as possible. We don't want to lose them now that they are within our grasp."

"I think we've lost them," he replied.

"No we haven't. Just hush a moment."

142

The three rescuers halted in the darkness, tilting their heads to one side. In the silence they heard a trapdoor spring softly into place.

"Did you hear that? Now we have lost them." Officer Kelly shook his fists.

"We will find the door," Donaldina said, taking out a candle and match. "Look for a weak panel—tap lightly along the walls."

Undaunted, the party searched for the secret door in the wall. Panel after panel was tested till the weak one was discovered and an entrance battered through.

"I wouldn't have believed it if I hadn't seen it with my own eyes," Officer Kelly said with surprise. "Can you imagine a hidden panel that turns out to be a door, but a little one at that!"

"Never mind. Just give me a hand and watch that the light doesn't go out." The missionary gathered up her long skirts and went into the adjoining passageway. It was pitch black. Only the candle flickering in her hand broke the darkness. A heavy scent of mildew and human waste flooded their nostrils. Donaldina might have turned back from the stench had it not been for her desire to save the young girl from slavery.

"You sure you want to go on, Miss Cameron?" Officer Kelly asked. "It smells awfully bad."

"We'll go on. She's got to be here somewhere."

"It sure is dark," the other officer said. "Looks like a maze of 100 different passageways, all going in a different direction."

Groping along in the silent darkness, they dis-

Gathering up her skirts, Donaldina boldly entered the darkened passageway

★ ★ ★ ★ ★ ★

143

1906 San Francisco earthquake destroys Chinatown

covered enclosed, empty rooms that in turn enclosed tiny cells. Somewhere, a secret pocket in the floor or wall held the slave girl. Such a labyrinth of corridors was not new to Donaldina. She had often led the police in perilous midnight raids to save a young woman from death or degradation. These rescues usually ended up in the city streets or on a country highway under the hot pursuit of a frenzied Tong man. But the good humor and determination of this woman had saved many a girl.

144

"We'll find her yet," Donaldina said, the candle-light splashing across her white head and twinkling dark eyes. "The Lord is with us. Now let's get on with it."

For six long hours they fingered the walls for hidden springs, lighting candle after candle, but found nothing. "I think it's time to call off the search," Officer Kelly finally said. "Hate to do this, ma'am, but we just ain't having any luck finding the hiding place."

"It's got to be here. She's locked in this maze of halls and rooms somewhere."

"We'll go back to the station and send in the second shift. Maybe they'll have better luck."

"I don't like to leave this one," Donaldina sighed. "Chiang spoke so sadly about her. And not more than 14 years old at that. What kind of life can she possibly have here? The girls I have helped are all good citizens now. Fine, upstanding women they are. And good Christians at that."

"Yes, ma'am."

"We'll go back down on the street and I'll wait while you go get the second crew. But first let me go up on the roof and check with the other girls. Perhaps they have seen something."

The two officers, dusty and sweating, came out of the dark passageways, stretching and twisting. " 'Tis a terrible think those Tongs do here. No respect for the ladies at all."

"You can see why I try so hard to help, Officer Kelly," Donaldina smoothed her skirts down and ran her hand through her hair. "Now just be patient a few moments more while I go up on the roof."

145

It was with a deep, refreshing breath that Doanldina pushed upon the rooftop door and stepped into the sunshine. "Going to be a fine day after all," she said to herself. Then, catching sight of the two Chinese girls she had earlier sent onto the roof to watch for any sign of the captors, she hurried forward.

One girl was peering over the side of the roof; the other saw Miss Cameron and ran towards her. "We see nothing but busy people," she said.

"You sure?"

"Oh, yes, Miss Cameron."

"What do you think has happened to Kum Lee?" Donaldina asked. "We found nothing inside but many hallways."

"Soon we know, I think," said the other girl, leaning against the edge of the roof. "Come look down there!"

Miss Cameron and the second girl joined her at the cornice edge. Down below, in the alley, two slave owners were involved in excited conversation, casting anxious glances upward. Suddenly, on an adjacent roof, a trapdoor lifted cautiously. A man's head appeared, moved about, and then dropped down into the hiding place once more.

"She's in the next building," the girls chanted eagerly.

"Yes, and we must hurry and find the opening before she is removed by way of the rooftop. Alert the officers below. I must find the dividing walls between the two buildings."

146

Her feet flew as she descended from the roof.

Estimating where the secret panel would be that connected the two structures, she moved her fingers along the tongue-and-groove, searching for the spring. "Oh Dear God, if you are at all about, please help me locate the right spot."

Nervously but with great care, she continued to touch the wall. A chill ran through her bones, and she shivered eagerly. "It's here! It's here!" Pushing forward on the weak spot in the panel, it shot back. Without hesitation, she stepped inside. There was nothing to be seen but a pile of empty rice bags and broken boxes under an old bunk.

"Have I missed the location?" she said aloud, continuing to move the rags about. No, she thought. The girl must be here. Working rapidly now lest the Tong men appear ahead the police, Donaldina lifted the last bag. There was the frightened girl, huddled in the corner, no bigger than a dog.

"Come," she said, taking her by the hand. "Come."

The frail Chinese girl could not understand the English words, but the intensity of Donaldina's speech was acknowledged. She crawled out from under the bunk and followed obediently.

Scrambling down the stairs came some Tong men, who had seen Donaldina with their new possession. "Stop," they shouted. "She belongs to us!"

"Quickly, my dear," the lady missionary said, all but dragging the young girl along. "Outside we will be safe."

At the bottom of the stairs the two Chinese girls from the mission were now yelling in Chinese to the slave girl, and the hearty words of Officer Kelly could be heard. There was also a dog or two barking, and several Chinese bystanders were shouting something unintelligible. It was hard to tell whose side they were on.

A patrol wagon arrived and Miss Cameron, the two mission girls, and Kum Lee were hustled inside. In short order they were joined by the shouting Tong men, who were still insisting that the girl belonged to them.

"Well, we'll see who she belongs to when we get to the station," Officer Kelly said, a wide grin crossing his massive face. "Glad to see you found her in time, Miss Cameron."

"So am I."

The noisy group arrived at the city jail and the officers gave a hasty report of the case. Donaldina appealed for temporary custody of the bewildered girl. Despite opposition from two attorneys serving the Tong men, the missionary was granted letters of guardianship, and Kum Lee was given a home in the Presbyterian Mission not twenty-four hours after arriving in San Francisco as a slave. With the aid of Donaldina Cameron the girl was saved from a life of slavery and introduced instead to the fundamentals and friendship of her Christian benefactor.

Throughout her forty years at the San Francisco Mission, Miss Cameron rescued hundreds of Chinese girls, literally snatching them away from their owners. The security of the Mission was the only ave-

nue of escape for the Chinese slave girl at that time. But the home was not merely a refuge. It was a Christian home, mothered by Donaldina. There was also a modern school, where English was taught by past graduates and Chinese was taught by a native woman from the Canton Mission. Domestic science was taught to the young women, and the girls themselves did all the work of the home. They grew into womanhood equipped with a fine moral background and with enough education to find a richer life in America.

All who found shelter in the home were challenged with writs of habeas corpus by their owners. Legal contests were sometimes long and drawn out. But the Mission seldom lost a case. Of course, Miss Cameron was at times reprimanded by the court for her tactics, and on one occasion they demanded her humble apology for an apparent misdemeanor.

As one newspaper reporter wrote of her during the early 1900s, "Clean and forceful in her mental processes, sure in her heart's purpose, fervent in her Christian spirit, strong in her self-effacement, and winsome in her natural attractions, this woman has equipment suited to meet the strange problems of her life work."

Indeed she did.

Asked one time why she labored among the Chinese, she declared: "I was born with a love for foreign races, and for the Chinese particularly. I am simply doing the work that I most enjoy, and there is no self-sacrifice in that."

INDEX

151